D0607248

"Pat Williams hits the bullseye again. Humility is the key ingredient of success and in this amazing book he inspires us to live, lead, and impact others with it. I loved this book and know you will too!"

Jon Gordon, Author of *The Energy Bus* and *The Carpenter*

"Pat Williams, in his magical way, highlights a rarely mentioned aspect of leadership and success—humility. His new book, *Humility*, contains many inspiring stories and insights that illustrate the value of being humble."

David Dombrowski, Boston Red Sox president of baseball operations

"The people I most admire in this world possess a truly humble sprit. This wonderful book by Pat Williams lays out some important principles that will be of value to every leader. It's that good."

Howie Roseman, Philadelphia Eagles executive vice president of football operations

"Pat Williams' book on humility speaks volumes on what it takes to succeed in life. It's a great book, and anyone in management needs to read every page."

Davey Johnson, Former Major League Baseball player and manager

"As an incredibly successful sports executive, husband, father, author, and motivational speaker, Pat Williams represents the best of leadership. His successes never come at the expense of others. His words inspire but never injure. He motivates through encouragement and allows his partners to learn and grow. And his example of a life well-lived is a blueprint for everyone. If ever there was a man who has had every right to brag, he doesn't. So I will for him. Read this book. To lead, you have to have followers. I've been honored to follow Pat Williams' leadership. Let him humbly lead you where you are meant to go!"

Chip Caray, Atlanta Braves broadcaster on Fox Sports South

"*Humility: The Secret Ingredient of Success* is a must-read. Pat Williams shares the stories of how world leaders, business leaders, sports leaders, and others have impacted the world through the combination of humility and confidence. Through his own combination of these two traits, Pat is able to pass on his wisdom to us, and he graciously shares the path which all of us can take in order to achieve these qualities."

Turner Gill, Liberty University head football coach

"In an age when mediocrities are elevated to celebrity, and strut an unearned arrogance before millions, this book could not be better timed. Pat Williams has gathered the wisdom and the examples of history to remind the old and instruct the young that genuine greatness travels in modest garb, that the conquest of one's own pride is the essential first step to achievement and leadership."

Mitch Daniels, Purdue University president

"When I was a boy my father told me that to become a successful baseball player I needed to learn humility. Now Pat Williams has written a book that proves, through story after story, that everything my father said is true. Humility is a learnable skill, essential to your success. Read this book and let it be your humility mentor and your success coach!"

Ferguson Jenkins, Major League Baseball Hall of Fame pitcher

"The books Pat Williams writes always cause me to think, reflect, and apply their life lessons. His latest work, *Humility*, is no exception. In fact, it may be his best one yet."

Sue Semrau, Florida State University head women's basketball coach

"This is an important book for our times. You'll love Pat's stories and insights. And the great surpass this—humility is a joy, not a burden."

John Eldredge, *New York Times* best-selling author of *Wild at Heart* and *Moving Mountains*

"I'm a major fan of humility. In his latest book, *Humility*, Pat Williams has captured many thoughts that I have on this valuable trait. This is a book I'd recommend to any friend, colleague, or player wh would like to add to their leadership toolbox."

Les Snead, Los Angeles Rams general manag

"If anyone can share the value of humility in Greatness it is Pat Williams. His accomplishments are many—as are his amazing books!—yet he maintains an unpretentious touch. The case here linking humility with success is undeniable and, best of all, includes tips on how all of us can build humility into our lives."

Don Yaeger, Nine-time *New York Times* bestselling author, author
Great Teams: 16 Things High Performing Organizations Do Differen

"Working in the television business for more than 25 years, I've come to appreciate the value of beir a good listener, team player, and always open to constructive criticism. I was also blessed to have a father and grandfather who taught me the true meaning of 'Minnesota Nice.' In this rewarding boo Pat Williams candidly shares his life stories too, telling us about the mistakes he made along the wa and how the lessons learned helped him to become one of the most well respected and successful executives in the sports world. Thanks, Pat, for a book I couldn't put down!"

Gretchen Carlson, Host of "The Real Story with Gretchen Carlson" on Fox New
bestselling author of *Getting Real*, former Miss America, and accomplished classical violin

"Narcissists aren't more successful leaders—they're just more visible. In the long run, the greatest teams and companies are led with humility. Pat Williams knows this from experience, and his book is full of inspiring examples of how to do it. If more leaders put his insights into action, we would a have better jobs and better lives."

Adam Grant, Wharton professor, *New York Times* bestselling author of *Originals* and *Give and Take*

"I can't say enough about this important book that Pat Williams has written about humility. His book is loaded with life examples that are very valuable guideposts and counsel on how we all shoul share our lives."

John Ashcroft, Attorney General of the United States (2001–200

"Pat Williams is an accomplished sports executive and prolific author. With *Humility*—to borrow a baseball analogy—he knocks it out of the park. Sports fans and business leaders alike can get something out of this book."

George H. McCaskey, Chicago Bears chairma

"Until I read this book I thought humility was important in life, but now I know it is indispensable. Every page was an eye-opener and vital for every aspiring leader to read and implement in their life.
Brian Kilmeade, *New York Times* bestselling author, host of "Fox & Friends" on Fox Nev

"Someone once told me that humility is not thinking less of yourself, but it is thinking more of God I believe you model that for all of us in the sports world and beyond. Thank you for your humble kindness and sincere words of encouragement to me. You remain such a blessing as I learn from you life, career, and sincerely humble spirit."

Bobby Evans, San Francisco Giants general manag

"I have always felt that the championship organizations I have observed or been a part of have been committed to continually learning—getting better every day. In order to learn, you must first be humble enough to be open to learning from others. Thus, humility is clearly an essential ingredient in leaders and organizations that sustain a championship level of success. Pat Williams, a true leader and learner, covers all of this with his consistent passion and unique insight in his new book, *Humility*. Read and lead."

Mark Shapiro, Toronto Blue Jays Baseball Club president and CE

Humility

The Secret Ingredient of Success

PAT WILLIAMS

WITH JIM DENNEY

SHILOH RUN PRESS
An Imprint of Barbour Publishing, Inc.

Print ISBN 978-1-63409-905-9

eBook Editions:
Adobe Digital Edition (.epub) 978-1-68322-026-8
Kindle and MobiPocket Edition (.prc) 978-1-68322-027-5

Cover photo: Bill Welch, Lightstock

Published by Shiloh Run Press, an imprint of Barbour Publishing, Inc., P.O. Box 719, Uhrichsville, Ohio 44683, www.shilohrunpress.com

Our mission is to publish and distribute inspirational products offering exceptional value and biblical encouragement to the masses.

ecpa Member of the
Evangelical Christian
Publishers Association

Printed in the United States of America.

Dedication

This book is dedicated to R. E. Littlejohn, Lamar Hunt, Jimmy Hewitt, Rich DeVos, and John Wooden, five men of note who consistently modeled humility in front of me and left a deep imprint on my life.

Acknowledgments

With deep appreciation I acknowledge the support and guidance of the following people who helped make this book possible:

Special thanks to Alex Martins, Dan DeVos, and Rich DeVos of the Orlando Magic.

Hats off to my associate Andrew Herdliska; my proofreader, Ken Hussar; and my ace typist, Fran Thomas.

Thanks also to my writing partner, Jim Denney, for his superb contributions in shaping this manuscript.

Hearty thanks also go to Kelly McIntosh and the entire Barbour team for their vision and insight, and for believing we had something important to say in these pages.

And finally, special thanks and appreciation go to my wife, Ruth, and to my wonderful and supportive family. They are truly the backbone of my life.

Contents

Foreword

Humility Has a New Publicist

The sports world is a world of big egos. It seems everywhere you look, you see people who are self-impressed with their own power and fame.

Now along comes Pat Williams, cofounder and senior vice president of the Orlando Magic, and he tells us that the key to success is what? *Humility*! No way — humility can't be a success trait, can it?

But read on. Pat will make a believer out of you. He'll prove to you that a humble attitude is, in fact, your most important business asset. And genuine humility is not just a personality trait some people are born with. It's a *learnable skill*.

As a youngster, I honed my pitching skills by going down to Terry's Coal and Ice Yard and pitching chunks of coal through the open doors of rolling boxcars — and I dreamed of being a pitcher in the major leagues. My father, Ferguson H. Jenkins, Sr., knew I had my sights set on a baseball career, and he told me, "Once you turn pro, keep your ego in check. Humility is a part of maturity. Learning to play the game and becoming a winning pitcher — that's only the beginning. To be a *real* winner, you have to stay humble."

My father was my greatest inspiration, and I was grateful that he could be there in Cooperstown when I was inducted into the Hall of Fame. His lessons in character and humility had as much to do with my being there as my baseball skills. Being selected for the Hall of Fame is not individual achievement, but an accomplishment I share with my teammates, family, and friends.

Humility is the ability to keep your accomplishments in perspective, so that you treat everybody with kindness and respect, from coaches to teammates to fans. Humility is the ability to accept criticism along with praise. No matter what you've accomplished on the field, there's always more to learn, so you have to stay humble.

I've known Pat Williams for — ohmigosh, has it been that long? — about fifty-five years. He was one of the first catchers I ever pitched to in pro baseball when we both played for the minor league Miami Marlins. Pat understands leadership, success, and humility. In this book, he'll prove that you can be humble and still be confident, assertive, and a winner.

These days, humility doesn't get much media attention. But humility has a new publicist, and his name is Pat Williams. If you want to achieve your dreams and make a difference in this world — read this book. Then humbly go out and achieve great things.

Ferguson Jenkins
Hall of Fame pitcher
Phoenix, Arizona
August 2016

Introduction

The X Factor

I know how great is the effort needed to convince the proud of the power and excellence of humility, an excellence which makes it soar above the summits of this world.
—Augustine of Hippo, *The City of God*

A few years ago, I interviewed Dr. Sheila Murray Bethel on my Orlando radio show. During our chat, she told me about a luncheon she attended in Washington, DC, in the late 1990s. The luncheon was hosted by Katharine Graham, the longtime publisher of *The Washington Post*. Mrs. Graham's parties and banquet events were known around the world for their stellar guest lists, which often included presidents, kings, and princesses.

Dr. Bethel told me, "I was seated next to Katharine Graham herself. I asked her, 'Mrs. Graham, you have hosted all the greatest leaders from around the world. What is the single most important trait of all great leaders?' Without hesitation, she said, 'The absence of arrogance.'

"She had stated it so simply, yet it was such a profound insight. As I watched Mrs. Graham conversing with others around the table, it struck me: *This woman is the perfect illustration of the trait she named—'absence of arrogance.'* Katharine Graham was one of the most powerful women in the world—yet it was her humility that defined her. Now, whenever I meet a great leader, I ask myself, 'Is this leader humble? Does he or she possess an absence of arrogance?' "

Dr. Bethel's description of Katharine Graham made me want to know more about this humble, powerful woman. I learned that she was born Katharine Meyer in 1917, the daughter of financier Eugene Meyer, who bought *The Washington Post* in a bankruptcy auction in 1933. Her mother, Agnes, was a friend of such personages as Albert Einstein, Eleanor Roosevelt, and the sculptor Rodin. Katharine began working for the *Post* in 1938, and two years later, she married Philip Graham, a law clerk for a Supreme Court justice.

Katharine's father made Philip publisher of the *Post* in 1946. Katharine and Philip became influential in Washington society and counted among their friends the likes of John F. Kennedy, Lyndon Johnson, and Henry Kissinger. Throughout their marriage, Philip Graham struggled with alcoholism and mood swings. In 1963, he entered a treatment center and was diagnosed with "manic depression" (now called bipolar disorder). In those days, mood-stabilizing medications were unknown. In August 1963, Philip's doctors allowed him to return home for the weekend. While Katharine was upstairs, she heard a deafening explosion downstairs. She rushed downstairs and found her husband dead from a self-inflicted shotgun blast.

After her husband's suicide, Katharine Graham

considered selling the *Post*—but she decided instead to succeed her husband as publisher. She called a meeting of top executives and reassured them that the *Post* would go on as before. "She looked ashen and devastated by her husband's horrible death," one editor, Osborn Elliott, said, "but she had the guts to convene the meeting. . . . That was the day before the funeral."[1]

At that time, the *Post* was one of several Washington, DC, newspapers, none of which was spoken of in the same breath as, say, *The New York Times*. Katharine Graham faced her first crisis as publisher in 1971 when the infamous Pentagon Papers were leaked to both *The New York Times* and *The Washington Post*. The Pentagon Papers revealed government deception regarding the Vietnam War, and the *Times* had been slapped with an injunction for publishing excerpts. If the *Post* also published excerpts, the newspaper's staff could be prosecuted under the Espionage Act, and the company could be financially crippled. Mrs. Graham risked the entire company for the people's right to know their government was lying to them. Though she later admitted she was "terrified" at the time, she approved the publication of the Pentagon Papers—and her decision was vindicated on First Amendment grounds by the Supreme Court.

She later showed similar courage when she gave executive editor Ben Bradlee and reporters Bob Woodward and Carl Bernstein approval to pursue the Watergate story. For a long time, the *Post* was the only newspaper covering the story—and Katharine Graham and her newspaper came under fire for that decision. Later, when the full story of Watergate came out and President Nixon resigned, she deflected any credit for her courageous decision to pursue the story, saying, "I never felt there was much choice."

But courage is always a choice. And so is humility.

In July 2001, while vacationing in Sun Valley, Idaho, Katharine Graham tripped and fell on a sidewalk, suffering a traumatic head injury. She died in a Boise hospital at age eighty-four. Again and again, people who knew Katharine Graham praised her for her courage and humility. President George W. Bush called her "a true leader and a true lady, steely yet shy, powerful yet humble." The *Post*'s resident political cartoonist, Herbert Block, said that Mrs. Graham was a leader "who didn't have any airs." Her longtime friend, Maryland lieutenant governor Kathleen Kennedy Townsend, described Katharine Graham as someone who was "very humble about who she was and what she accomplished."

The day after Mrs. Graham's death, the *Post* headline read A PIONEER WITH COURAGE, INFLUENCE AND HUMILITY. In the story, Pulitzer-winning feature writer Steve Twomey wrote that, by her courage, Katharine Graham had changed journalism forever "because, facing the powerful opposition of the federal government, she told her editors to publish. Twice."

Twomey also noted, "She was gutsy, so many said, yet never trumpeted the fact. Her wealth and influence were great, but wielded with grace. . . . Few lives blend so many traits so seamlessly."[2]

Katharine Graham's funeral was held at Washington National Cathedral. She was eulogized by Senator John Danforth, who is an ordained Episcopal priest. He said:

> Of the many words written this last week, one sentence deserves special attention. It's from Katharine Graham's obituary in the Post: "Mrs. Graham was often described as the most powerful woman in the world, a notion she dismissed out of hand". . . . That is an astonishing statement in this town. . . .
>
> St. Paul tells us, "Do nothing from selfish ambition or conceit, but in humility regard others as better than yourselves. Let each of you look not to your own interests, but to the interests of others."
>
> That is the way believers are supposed to live. . . . It is very biblical and very true that "every one who exalts himself will be humbled, and he who humbles himself will be exalted." That is a text for all of us. It was lived by Katharine Graham.[3]

After Sheila Murray Bethel told me about her encounter with Katharine Graham, and after I did my own research into Mrs. Graham's life, I reflected on her statement that the single most important leadership trait is "the absence of arrogance." I thought back through history. Could I think of any person of true greatness who was not also a person of deep humility? George Washington, Abraham Lincoln, Gandhi, Martin Luther King Jr., Rosa Parks, Ronald Reagan, Nelson Mandela, Mother Teresa—they certainly *seemed* to be people with an "absence of arrogance." Yet they strongly believed in themselves, their cause, and their goals. Clearly an "absence of arrogance" was not an absence of confidence. A leader can have great self-confidence and still be humble.

Next, I thought of all the leaders in history who were notoriously arrogant and narcissistic. I thought of all the dictators and tyrants who had inflicted so much suffering on the world—Nero, Napoléon Bonaparte, Hitler, Mussolini, Stalin, Mao, Pol Pot, Saddam Hussein, Qaddafi, and on and on. They all cultivated a cult of personality around themselves and didn't hesitate to slaughter millions just to maintain their power and privilege. Arrogance was the central pillar of their character, the trait that defined them. For a while, they held power and seemed successful—but history curses their memory.

I have written books and given speeches on leadership and success. Wherever I go, the number one question people ask is, "What is the recipe for success?" Most of the ingredients for success are familiar to us all—talent, passion, the courage to take risks, perseverance, and an intense focus on our goals.

But there is one ingredient that is rarely mentioned when people discuss leadership and success. Katharine Graham identified this invisible "X factor" as an "absence of arrogance." In other words, *humility*.

You might say, "Humility is fine for a saint like Mother Teresa—but I want success in the business world." Or, "I want to be successful in the performing arts." Or, "I want a successful government career." I'm here to tell you that the secret ingredient of success—however you define it, in whatever field you seek it—is this trait called humility.

And I can prove it.

For years, ever since Dr. Bethel shared this insight with me, I've been studying humility as a crucial component of success and leadership, and my files bulge with stories and insights about the power of humility to generate success. The longer I've lived and the more I've learned, the more I'm convinced that humility may be the most important trait any human being can possess. As Charles R. Swindoll once observed, "If I were to boil down all the characteristics of greatness to a single word, it would be humility."

In the coming pages, I'm going to introduce you to the rewards of humility—and the high cost of arrogance. I'll take you on a tour of the history of humble greatness and introduce you to people whose success was amplified by their humility. I'll show you how to balance great confidence with deep humility. I'll help you avoid the trap of false humility. And I'll show you how to recruit talented, humble people to your organization.

If you have read all the books, attended all the seminars, and heard all the motivational talks about success, but the success you want still eludes you—I think this book will introduce you to the "X Factor," the missing ingredient you have been searching for. Once you understand the role of humility in making people and organizations successful, your world will begin changing for the better.

It's time to add the secret sauce of humility to your recipe for success. Turn the page, and come with me. Let me be your humble guide to a lifetime of greatness.

1

The Price of Arrogance,
the Rewards of Humility

With great humility comes great success.
—Hip-hop artist Yelawolf

In 1965, the Philadelphia Phillies hired me as general manager of the Phillies' farm club in Spartanburg, South Carolina. After my first season, the Western Carolinas League named me Executive of the Year. It was quite an honor for a twenty-five-year-old in his first season as a sports executive—and it went straight to my head. My hat size had swelled into triple digits, and I was sure I'd soon be flooded with job offers from the big leagues.

Those offers never came in, but I continued to wear expensive suits and drive a big Oldsmobile Toronado with a Super Rocket V-8 engine. The following year, we again packed in the fans and even brought home a championship. Once again, the league named me Executive of the Year. The front office in Philadelphia was keeping an eye on me, and in September 1966, Phillies owner Bob Carpenter called me. At first, I was excited—I was sure he was calling to offer me the job of general manager of the Philadelphia Phillies.

But no. He told me he wanted me to start a brand-new Phillies farm club in Reading, Pennsylvania.

I groaned inwardly. Didn't he know what I had accomplished in my short time in Spartanburg? Why should I go to Reading and start from scratch? If it hadn't been for my swelled head, I would have been flattered that Mr. Carpenter had so much faith in me.

The Phillies flew me up for the big meeting. I arrived at the Phillies ballpark at Twenty-First and Lehigh and strode into the owner's office suite. It was a high-level meeting with Bob Carpenter himself, general manager John Quinn, and farm director Paul Owens, and other front-office execs. Mr. Carpenter laid out the offer.

"Pat," he said, "we're very pleased with the progress you've made in Spartanburg. To show you how much confidence we have in you, we want to offer you this big opportunity in Reading." He laid out the plan and told me what the job would entail.

I'm ashamed and embarrassed at what I did next—and I remember it as clearly as if it happened yesterday. "I don't see how this would be a good career move for me," I said. "I'm ready to move up in baseball. Why should I jeopardize everything I've accomplished by moving to a little Podunk town in Pennsylvania? How do I know it's really a baseball town?" For the next few minutes, I proceeded to dig a hole with my big, fat, arrogant mouth.

As soon as I started talking, the smile faded from Mr. Carpenter's face. I could have simply thanked him for his generous offer. I could have said I wanted to honor my commitment to my boss in Spartanburg, Mr. R. E. Littlejohn. But no, I had to play the big shot—and I had just blown my baseball career sky-high.

When I returned to Spartanburg, Mr. Littlejohn told me that the Phillies organization had canceled my salary and health benefits. If Mr. Littlejohn wanted to keep me on at his own expense, he was free to do so—but the Phillies had washed their hands of me.

A few weeks later, my lifelong friend Ruly Carpenter (Bob Carpenter's son) called me on the phone. "What was that performance all about?" he said. "My dad was offering you the opportunity of a lifetime, and you threw it in his face. I've known you most of my life, and you've always been a level-headed guy. What got into you?"

"I don't know, Ruly. I really don't know."

The Spartanburg Phillies of 1966 had a great season. Our promotions drew 173,000 fans in a town of 46,000 people, and I expected to win the Outstanding Minor League Baseball Executive of the Year award from *The Sporting News*. The award went to someone else. Only then did I realize that *The Sporting News* had probably consulted with the Phillies front office before making a selection. My arrogance had cost me the award.

I went to my home in Wilmington, Delaware, for Christmas. Mr. Carpenter, who also lived in Wilmington, called and asked me over to his home for a chat. I knew what he wanted. I had known Bob

Carpenter most of my life. I had been in his home and eaten at his table many times. He had graciously given me my start in baseball and had offered me a chance for real advancement—and I had treated his kindness with contempt.

I arrived at his palatial home, and he ushered me into his study. He didn't waste any words. "Pat," he said sternly, "what have they been feeding you down there in Spartanburg?"

"Sir?"

"As long as I've known you, you've been a bright, ambitious, well-mannered young man. But that's not the young man I saw in Philadelphia a few months ago."

"Sir," I said weakly, "I can't even explain it to myself. I can only say I'm sorry."

Mr. Carpenter accepted my apology, but I had ruined my chances of moving up in the Phillies organization. And I had learned a powerful lesson. I had paid the high price of arrogance.

Since then, I have learned not only the high price of arrogance but the vast rewards of humility.

Fueled by Arrogance

For years, golfer Tiger Woods was an Orlando Magic season-ticket holder. His seats were on the floor, front row, directly across from the visitors' bench. Ever since the team was founded, I have stood in the tunnel, directly behind the visitors' bench, so at every home game, I would look across the floor and see

Tiger in his sneakers, blue jeans, sweater, and Nike baseball cap. He'd always watch the game intently and silently. Even when the crowd was going crazy, cheering and waving towels, Tiger was motionless— and seemingly emotionless. He never moved. He was focused on the game.

I never had a conversation with him, never introduced myself. It was clear that he was there to watch the game, not to talk. I contented myself with observing.

On one occasion, I visited the Isleworth Country Club near Orlando to attend an NBA event. It was a miserable, blistering-hot day—95 degrees with 100 percent humidity. While driving on the club grounds, I noticed a man running in the opposite direction. He was shirtless, and his skin glistened with sweat. I turned my car around and came back for another look. Sure enough, it was Tiger Woods.

It was doubly amazing because I knew the Tiger had just won a golf tournament the previous day in another state. He had flown into Orlando and was putting himself through a punishing workout in the blazing heat.

Watching him, I thought, *Now there's a young man who has it all together. He's always disciplined, whether he's watching a basketball game, or working out, or playing golf.* Like most sports fans following Tiger's career, I had bought the image—and I was unaware that behind that image was another Tiger Woods, a very different Tiger Woods.

Eldrick Tont "Tiger" Woods is among the most successful golfers of all time, and he has been one of the highest-paid athletes in the world. He turned pro at age twenty in mid-1996. By April 1997 he had won the 1997 Masters with a record-breaking twelve strokes, taking home a princely $486,000 prize. Two months later, he was ranked first in the world. He continued to dominate professional golf for the next dozen years, and in 2009 he became the first athlete in any sport to accumulate more than $1 billion (before taxes) in career earnings.

That same year, on November 25, 2009, the roof fell in on Tiger Woods. A supermarket tabloid published a story claiming Tiger Woods had cheated on his wife with a New York City nightclub manager. In the wee hours of the morning of November 27, Tiger got behind the wheel of his Cadillac Escalade, roared out of his driveway onto the street, and then drove through a hedge, colliding with a tree. He was later treated for facial lacerations. There was widespread media speculation about the incident, but Tiger would only say that it was a "private matter" and that his wife had helped him out of the car after the accident.

It became clear that Tiger had engaged in a series of extramarital affairs. With each new allegation, Tiger issued another statement, apologizing to his wife and fans. On December 11, he announced he was taking "an indefinite break from professional golf." A number of companies ended their endorsement relationship with him. A study published in December 2009 estimated that shareholders in those companies lost up to $12 billion due to Tiger Woods's affairs.[4]

Tiger's "indefinite break from professional golf" lasted until April 2010, and he and his wife divorced four months later. Under the terms of their divorce agreement, Tiger paid his wife at least $750 million dollars—three-quarters of a billion dollars—for a guarantee that she would never speak or write about Tiger's twenty or so alleged affairs.[5] That's a steep price to pay for silence—and for arrogance.

When Tiger Woods returned to the game, it became clear that there was a side of his personality most of us had missed. In fact, Tiger had kept it carefully hidden. A CBS News editorial by sportswriter Mike Freeman suggested that we were just now discovering the *real* Tiger Woods—and the headline identified the trait that defined the golfing phenom: WOODS SHOWS ARROGANCE IN HOGAN COMPARISON.

Freeman wrote that during a press briefing after returning to the Masters, "Woods compared himself to [golf] legend Ben Hogan, who missed extensive time due to a car crash that nearly killed him." Hogan and his wife, Valerie, were driving on a fog-shrouded bridge in Texas in February 1949 when a Greyhound bus loomed out of the mist. Cars didn't have seatbelts in those days, so Hogan threw himself across his wife to protect her. The car collided head-on with the bus, and Valerie suffered only minor injuries. Hogan suffered a double fracture of the pelvis, a broken collarbone, an ankle fracture, and near-fatal blood clots. He spent two months in the hospital and a year away from professional golf.

"Hogan missed time because he was a valiant hero who saved his wife," Freeman observed. "Woods missed time after cheating on his wife with cocktail waitresses and porn stars. Woods continually putting his name and Hogan's together in that way is like an actor who plays a war hero saying he knows the pain of war. Yet that's Woods, and clearly such arrogance, rightly and wrongly, continues to fuel him."[6]

Over time, Tiger dropped steadily in the rankings, suffering a 107-week winless streak. Except for a brief time in 2013 when he temporarily regained his focus and his dominance, he has never regained the consistency he once enjoyed. It was arrogance and hubris that made him believe he could get away with marital infidelities on a grand scale and never have to pay the price. And it was that same arrogance and hubris that caused him to compare his escapades to the heroism of the great Ben Hogan. His arrogance cost him millions in endorsements and turned him into joke fodder for late-night comedians.

There is always a high price to pay for arrogance.

THE ARCHETYPE OF ARROGANT GREED

What does the name Dennis Kozlowski mean to you?

If you're like most people, that name seems vaguely

familiar but you can't quite place where you heard it before. But if I said to you, "Do you remember news stories about a corporate CEO who had a $6,000 shower curtain in his $30 million New York apartment? Do you remember the story of how he threw a $2 million party on the island of Sardinia for his wife's fortieth birthday—a party featuring Roman togas, a private concert by Jimmy Buffett, and an ice sculpture of Michelangelo's *David* that, well, fountained Stolichnaya vodka?"

"Oh!" you're probably saying. "*That* Dennis Kozlowski!"

He grew up poor and humble in Newark, New Jersey, with a hardscrabble work ethic. In his youth, he held two or three jobs at a time, working at a pharmacy and a car wash while also playing guitar in a garage band. He started as an accountant with Tyco, a small New Hampshire manufacturer in 1975, when he was twenty-nine years old. By 1992, he had worked his way up to the corner office. As CEO, he expanded the company through mergers and acquisitions, taking Tyco from a $40 million company to a $40 billion conglomerate.

With success came arrogance. Kozlowski became famous for his $100 million annual salary and a matching lifestyle of extravagance. *The New York Times* said Kozlowski "reigned as the archetype of avarice."[7] He purchased estates in Boca Raton and Nantucket. He threw a $2 million birthday party for his wife—and billed Tyco International for half the tab. That party became known as the "Tyco Roman Orgy."

In 2005, a jury convicted Kozlowski of twenty-two counts of grand larceny, conspiracy, and securities fraud. In essence, he was convicted of looting Tyco of hundreds of millions of dollars and living large while robbing stockholders of return on investment. He received a sentence of up to twenty-five years in prison but was released in January 2014 after serving six years. While in prison, Kozlowski—who had reportedly hauled in as much as $170 million in salary and bonuses one year—earned a dollar a day mopping floors and serving meals to fellow prisoners.

To this day, Kozlowski maintains his innocence. In an interview on the CBS-TV newsmagazine *60 Minutes*, Kozlowski told Morley Safer, "I was a guy sitting in a courtroom who made $100 million a year. And I think a juror sitting there just would have to say, 'All that money, he musta done somethin' wrong.' I think. . .it's as simple as that."[8] Kozlowski's plunge from the penthouse to the big house prompted CBS News to ask: "Why does a man who struggled so hard [to achieve success]. . .become so careless and stupid and arrogant?"[9]

An ancient version of Dennis Kozlowski was the Macedonian conqueror-king known as Alexander the Great. His arrogance was so great, he considered himself a god in human form. Much has been written of Alexander's accomplishments. As a soldier, he earned his first command at age sixteen, won his first battle at age eighteen, and succeeded his father, Philip of Macedon, to the throne by age twenty. By age twenty-six, he ruled the eastern half of the ancient world. By age thirty, he had conquered nearly *all* the known world and had spread Greek culture throughout those conquered lands.

Alexander's victories only confirmed his confidence in his own godhood. When he was a child, his mother had told him of a prophecy that he would be worshipped as a god. Now, here he was, achieving godlike success. Alexander surrounded himself with yes-men, who only praised him and never dared to argue with his claim to be a god.

One day, when Alexander and his generals were eating, drinking, and celebrating victory in Samarkand, an ancient city in central Asia, Alexander's old friend Cleitus got into an argument with him. Cleitus told Alexander that he was no god and that all his accomplishments were due to the greatness of Alexander's father, King Philip. Drunk and enraged, Alexander hurled a javelin at his old friend. The javelin went through Cleitus's heart, and Alexander's friend fell dead.

In 323 BC, Alexander was in his headquarters in the palace of Nebuchadnezzar in the ancient city of Babylon. He and his generals were planning a new campaign, the conquest of Arabia. After a day and a night of reveling and drinking, Alexander developed a fever, which worsened over the next few days. Alexander died after eleven days of intense suffering. The cause of his death is unknown, and speculation ranges from disease (malaria or meningitis) to a lifestyle of heavy drinking (acute pancreatitis) to murder (slow poisoning with plant toxins). So the man who thought he was a god died in agony at age thirty-two.

In *Power Ambition Glory: The Stunning Parallels between Great Leaders of the Ancient World and Today*, Steve Forbes and John Prevas tell us that "Alexander is a cautionary example for today's leaders." They explain:

> *For Alexander it was all about conquest—"acquisitions" in today's corporate world. He was willing to pay whatever price was necessary to achieve his goal of nothing short of conquering the world. . . .*
>
> *Though idolized in the West, he is not always viewed in the East as an enlightened leader. . . . [He brought] suffering, enslavement, and death to millions. Some of the countries that Alexander subjugated nearly twenty-four hundred years ago—Iran, Afghanistan, and Pakistan—make up today's "terrorist belt," areas in which anti-Western sentiment is at its most virulent. There, Alexander, or Iskander as he is called,*

is often portrayed as an early example of Western cultural arrogance and exploitation. . . .

Leaders like Alexander often. . . come to believe that they alone know what is best. They stop seeking, listening, and learning. They become rigid, authoritative, and no longer receptive to feedback from subordinates in their own organizations or the markets. When this happens, a corporate version of hardening of the arteries sets in, the flow of fresh ideas to the top is slowed, and the end is usually close.[10]

Tiger Woods thought he could cheat on his wife and there would never be any consequences to pay. Dennis Kozlowski thought he could cheat his investors and live like a Roman emperor and there would never be any consequences to pay. Alexander the Great thought himself a god, and he died an agonizing death at age thirty-two.

There is always a high price to pay for arrogance.

HUMILITY—OR HUMILIATION?

Figure skater Michelle Kwan is a two-time Olympic medalist and a five-time world champion. From age ten to twenty-one, Kwan trained under legendary competitive skater Frank Carroll—but in late 2001,

Kwan fired her longtime coach, saying, "When I was younger, the coach was pretty much the skater. You did whatever he said. As I've gotten older and grown more independent, I think for myself, and that's how it should be."[11]

Entrepreneur Steven K. Scott recalls watching Michelle Kwan compete in the 2002 Winter Olympics. Kwan, the reigning world champion, was heavily favored to win the gold in the figure skating finals. Scott recalls that, the morning before the event, Kwan told Katie Couric on *The Today Show* that she had fired her longtime coach and didn't need a coach to guide her.

Hearing that, Scott turned to his wife and said, "She's not going to win!"

"Why do you say that?"

"Pride has become the basis of her decision," Scott said. "She's going to have a fall."

That night, Michelle Kwan went out to perform in one of the most important figure skating events of her career—and she fell. As a result, Scott said, "the crown jewel of her career, an Olympic gold medal, was lost."

But there was another American skater preparing to perform that night—sixteen-year-old Sarah Hughes. As she awaited her turn on the ice, Hughes looked into the eyes of her coach, listening intently to every word of instruction and encouragement he gave her. She drank it all in, then nodded, smiled, and skated out onto the rink.

Watching on television, Scott said to his wife, "Watch this—she's going to give the performance of her life."

"How do you know?"

"Look how humble she is. She's soaking up her coach's advice like a sponge. . . . She's just going to go out there, have a good time doing what she loves most, and try to perform like never before."

And she did. In fact, she attempted a quadruple jump—a skating move so difficult and risky that no woman skater had ever attempted it in competition. Hughes executed the quadruple jump perfectly—not once, but twice—and won the gold.

That ancient font of wisdom, King Solomon, warned, "Pride goes before destruction, a haughty spirit before a fall" (Proverbs 16:18). I'm not sure King Solomon had a literal fall on ice in mind when he wrote those words, but they were certainly fulfilled during the 2002 Winter Olympics. It's ironic but true: Pride can bring you down. Humility can elevate you to the winner's circle and put a gold medal around your neck.

One of the greatest dangers we face in our attempt to remain humble is that the very moment we notice we are humble, we become proud of our humility—and in that instant, our humility evaporates. C. S. Lewis, in *The Screwtape Letters*, depicts an experienced devil named Screwtape writing to his inexperienced nephew Wormwood about ways to tempt human beings into the sin of arrogant pride. Referring to the human victim as a "patient," Screwtape writes:

> *Your patient has become humble; have you drawn his attention to the fact? All virtues are less formidable to us once the man is aware that he has them, but this is specially true of humility. Catch him at the moment when he is really poor in spirit and smuggle into his mind the gratifying reflection, "By jove! I'm being humble," and almost immediately pride—pride at his own humility—will appear. If he awakes to the danger and tries to smother this new form of pride, make him proud of his attempt—and so on, through as many stages as you please. But don't try this too long, for fear you awake his sense of humour and proportion, in which case he will merely laugh at you and go to bed.*[12]

Humility may be defined as "a modest and realistic view of one's own importance." Someone once said that humility doesn't mean thinking less of yourself. It just means thinking of yourself less. In other words, a genuinely humble person doesn't say, "I'm worthless," but instead says, "I'm no more important than anyone else—and no less important, either."

Genuine humility has great value in the world of

leadership and success. Humble people treat others as equals, which creates bonds of trust, respect, and loyalty. Humble people don't claim to know everything; so they are teachable and eager to listen and learn. Humble people are better team players because they are not riddled with insecurity, jealousy, or envy. Humble people are willing to set aside their egos to achieve a goal or dream that is bigger than themselves. As a result, humble people usually accomplish much more than arrogant people.

Humble people don't confuse humility with humiliation. A humiliated person feels weak and enslaved; a humble person feels strong to serve others. A humiliated person feels helpless and hopeless; a humble person feels helpful and hopeful. A humiliated person feels powerless and dishonored; a humble person feels empowered and dignified. Humiliation tears down; humility builds up. Humiliation is a tragedy; humility is a choice.

Genuine humility is one of the greatest strengths a leader can possess. Humble leaders are strong enough to listen to other points of view, strong enough to admit mistakes and learn from them, strong enough to celebrate the achievements and successes of others, and strong enough to surround themselves with talented people without feeling threatened or diminished.

A "Soft" Virtue with Solid Benefits

Let me put it bluntly: humility is a strength; arrogance is weakness.

That statement saws across the grain of our culture, which celebrates arrogance and scorns humility. But there's a US Marine who backs up this claim. His name is Donovan Campbell. After graduating from Princeton, Campbell wanted to serve his country and learn real-world leadership skills, so he enlisted in the Marines. He served in Iraq, where he commanded a forty-man infantry platoon called Joker One. He and his platoon were posted in Ramadi, the capital of the Sunni-dominated Anbar province. There, Campbell and his platoon endured some of the most brutal and hellish combat of the Iraq War. Campbell wrote about his experiences in a 2009 book, *Joker One*, and followed it with a 2013 book of leadership lessons, *The Leader's Code*.

The virtue of humility, Campbell says, "serves as a necessary counterbalance to a driving sense of mission." Leaders can sometimes become so wrapped up in their drivenness and their passion for their goals that they lose perspective. He explains:

> *Passionate leaders who pursue their*
> *mission without humility. . .risk*
> *destroying that which they would save.*
> *They are prone to justifying any means*
> *that will bring about their noble end—*

*even if that means goes against all
commonly accepted human decency. With
no one to check them, and with no desire
to be checked, a little evil for a great good
becomes an acceptable trade-off. Once a
little evil is acceptable, then the dam is
breached and a lot of evil becomes routine.
Those who stand in the way, be they
individuals or whole classes of people,
become acceptable losses.[13]*

As examples, Campbell cites French revolutionary leader Robespierre, who beheaded thousands of people in the name of "liberty, equality, and fraternity"; Josef Stalin, who starved and slaughtered tens of millions to achieve his Marxist workers' paradise; and Cambodian dictator Pol Pot, who slaughtered a third of the Cambodian population, telling them, "To keep you is no benefit, to destroy you is no loss." Campbell adds, "The more an arrogant leader seeks to bring heaven to earth, the greater the likelihood that they will create a terrestrial hell."

Humility is the essential moral firewall that prevents a passionate leader from becoming a ruthless tyrant. Humble leaders recognize their own limitations, and instead of surrounding themselves with sycophants and yes-men who praise everything they do, they surround themselves with honest, faithful friends who will tell them the hard truths and keep them from becoming too full of themselves.

Campbell reminds us of the ancient wisdom from Proverbs 27:6 (KJV): "Faithful are the wounds of a friend." Humble leaders seek out and listen to the words of faithful friends, even if those words are painful to hear. So humility keeps leaders in check and prevents them from becoming so fanatical about their mission that they end up destroying their mission.

Donovan Campbell also points out that humble leaders learn from their mistakes, while arrogant leaders only shift the blame for their mistakes. Because leaders make a lot of decisions, they invariably make a lot of mistakes—more mistakes than the average person. Arrogant leaders, whose decisions are never questioned and their words never challenged, keep making the same mistakes over and over again, because they never learn from their failures and misjudgments. Only humble leaders learn and grow from their mistakes.

Campbell concludes, "The 'soft' virtue of humility, therefore, has some very 'hard' practical consequences."[14]

CONQUERING THE ARROGANCE WITHIN

These two qualities—humility and arrogance—seem worlds apart, but they are practically two sides of the same human coin. Even in our moments of deepest humility, we can succumb to pride, selfishness, and egotism. Humility is a choice—and so is arrogance. The wild beast of arrogance always lurks within us—because arrogance and self-centeredness are our natural animal state. The beast of arrogance can only be subdued by a more powerful, more spiritual force: the character strength of humility. We must continually choose an attitude of humility—or we will choose arrogance by default.

There are few experiences more enjoyable than meeting a truly humble person. When you are in the presence of humility, you know that you will be received, listened to, and accepted for who you are. A truly humble person won't try to impress you, manipulate you, judge you, criticize you, or put you in your place. Humble people are safe to be around. You can relax. You can be yourself.

Humility is a gift we give to other people. Ironically, arrogance makes us seem small and pathetic. Humility is what makes people great.

George Stevens was an American film director, producer, and screenwriter. He won Best Director Oscars for *A Place in the Sun* (1951) and *Giant* (1956). He also directed such landmark films as *Shane* (1953), *The Diary of Anne Frank* (1959), and *The Greatest Story Ever Told* (1965). Stevens began his Hollywood career as a cameraman on Laurel and Hardy short films and soon began directing minor comedies for Universal and RKO studios. During World War II, Stevens served with the Army Signal Corps, heading a special combat motion picture unit. He waded ashore at Normandy on D-Day, carrying a camera instead of a gun. He was on hand to film the liberation of Paris—and the liberation of the Dachau concentration camp.

The footage Stevens shot at Dachau shocked the conscience of the world—and his experience during the liberation of Dachau profoundly changed George Stevens as a filmmaker and as a human being. It revealed to him not only the arrogance of the Nazis but the horrible beast of arrogance that lurks within us all.

He recalled the day he walked through the gates of the concentration camp and encountered a victim of the camp, a starving man who was unable to see. The man grabbed at Stevens and begged him for food. At that moment, Stevens confessed, he experienced the same arrogant hatred the Nazis must have felt. Instead of feeling compassion for the starving beggar, Stevens said, "I abhor him, I want him to keep his hands off me. And the reason I want him to keep his hands off me is because I see myself capable of arrogance and brutality to keep him off me. That's a fierce thing, to discover within yourself that which you despise the most in others."[15]

The films George Stevens made after World War II were quite different from the films he made before the war. Instead of trivial comedies, he focused on gritty dramas that revealed the human condition and celebrated the human spirit. After discovering to his horror the arrogance that lurked within him, he made a conscious commitment to choose humility, and to use the medium of motion pictures to battle the arrogance and brutality of the world.

So beware of this arrogant beast that lurks within us all, this creature called Ego. Avoid the high cost of arrogance, because when that bill comes due, none of us can afford it. Instead, seek the rewards of humility. In the next chapter, I'll introduce you to some people who found success through humility—and I'll show you the rewards they earned.

2

A Short History of Humility

*Humility's strength is hidden, obscured by our
blindness and the age of arrogance in which we live.*
—Educator David J. Bobb[16]

At Yeatman's Cove, on the riverfront of downtown Cincinnati, stands a large bronze statue of Lucius Quinctius Cincinnatus, the namesake of the city. His hand is outstretched, holding a bundle of rods with an ax in the middle, symbolizing the authority of a Roman leader. His other hand grips the handle of a farmer's plow. These are important symbols.

Cincinnatus lived five centuries before Christ and was once an influential aristocrat and a revered general in the army of Rome. But he had removed himself from the city to live in humble circumstances, working as a farmer. When Rome was invaded by neighboring tribes, the people of Rome begged him to return and offered him the authority of a supreme dictator. Cincinnatus agreed and became the ruler of Rome. He organized a counterattack against the invaders, and within two weeks, Cincinnatus defeated the invaders. Once the crisis was over, Cincinnatus resigned and returned to his farm. To this day, Cincinnatus is viewed as a role model of civic virtue—the only Roman dictator who willingly, humbly relinquished power.

President Harry S. Truman was a great admirer of Cincinnatus. He once said, "If a man can accept a situation in a place of power with the thought that it is only temporary, he comes out all right. But when he thinks that he is the *cause* of the power, that can be ruination."[17]

In the closing days of his presidency, Truman wrote a letter to his cousin, Ethel Noland, reflecting on the power he had wielded as president, and which he would soon relinquish: "Alexander the great, Augustus Caesar, Genghis Khan, Louis XIV, Napoléon, nor any other of the great historical figures have the power or the world influence of the President of the USA. It bears down on a country boy. But I'm coming home January 20, 1953, and will, I hope, pull a Cincinnatus, who was old G. Washington's ideal."[18]

It's true: Cincinnatus was a role model for "old G. Washington." In fact, General George Washington passed up an opportunity to become king of the United States. In October 1781, after defeating the British forces at Yorktown, Virginia, Washington set up headquarters in a house on the banks of the Hudson. Peace talks had begun in Paris. The thirteen colonies were negotiating with Great Britain, demanding recognition as an independent nation. Washington awaited news from the peace conference but kept his Continental Army ready just in case.

In May 1782, one of Washington's most loyal friends and patriotic officers, Colonel Lewis Nicola, wrote a letter on behalf of himself and other high-ranking officers. Stating that a democratic government would be unstable, Nicola urged Washington to consider becoming the head of a British-style constitutional monarchy. Under Nicola's plan, Washington would become "King George I"—and Nicola and his comrades would back him as king.

A horrified Washington replied that he felt a "mixture of great surprise and astonishment" at the notion that he might become America's first king. "You could not have found a person to whom your schemes are more disagreeable," Washington said, imploring Nicola to "banish these thoughts from your Mind, and never communicate, as from yourself, or any one else, a sentiment of the like Nature."[19]

Those are the heartfelt words of a genuinely humble man. If not for Washington's humility, the American Revolution might have produced a very different result.

A Nation Carved by Humility

To see how America might have turned out under "King George I," we have only to look at the French Revolution (1789 to 1799). While the American Revolution produced a stable democratic republic with Washington as its first president, the French Revolution produced a new French Empire, with Napoléon Bonaparte as its first emperor. America under President Washington experienced peace and prosperity; France under Napoléon experienced war, terror, and misery.

Washington is the only president who never campaigned for public office. He was elected to two terms and was unopposed both times. He could have easily won a third term but refused the honor. When King George III of England heard that Washington had freely relinquished power, he was astounded. King George said that if Washington kept his promise and walked away from the presidency, he would be "the greatest character of the age." Washington relinquished power and is remembered as the father of a nation. Napoléon craved power, waging endless wars of conquest, and he was forced into exile. He is remembered as a tyrant. Shortly before he died, Napoléon reflected bitterly, "They wanted me to be another Washington."[20]

During Washington's lifetime, artist Jean-Antoine Houdon sculpted an image that stands in the rotunda of the Virginia state capital in Richmond. It depicts Washington in civilian clothing, standing in front of his plow—America's Cincinnatus. After Washington's death, the poet Lord Byron eulogized him as "the Cincinnatus of the West."

What kind of man was George Washington? Was he always such a humble and self-effacing man? No. Several Washington biographers refer to his "youthful arrogance"—but they also record that Washington learned humility through setbacks and sufferings, especially during his involvement in the French and Indian War, 1754 to 1758.[21] Those setbacks included his capture by the French at Fort Necessity in 1754 and his role in planning the disastrous Braddock Expedition of 1755.

Twenty years later, in April 1775, the king's troops entered Lexington and Concord, Massachusetts, seeking to disarm the rebellious Massachusetts militia. This event touched off the American Revolution. In June, the Continental Congress chose Washington as commander in chief of the newly formed Continental Army. His job was to organize the motley militias of the various states into a single, cohesive fighting force.

By this time, the forty-three-year-old Washington had found that perfect balance between confidence and humility. He humbly accepted the responsibility that the Continental Congress conferred on him, saying, "I this day declare with the utmost sincerity, I do not think myself equal to the command I am honored with." Refusing compensation, Washington began assembling the new Continental Army.[22]

Historian David McCullough tells us that the Continental Congress chose Washington because of his character, integrity, and humility. "They knew the kind of man he was," McCullough explains. "He was a man people would follow. And as events would prove, he was a man whom some—a few—would follow through hell."[23]

Washington's quiet, humble nature made him extremely popular with his troops. He battled the British relentlessly, finally forcing General Charles

Cornwallis to surrender on October 19, 1781. Two months later, Washington resigned his commission and began his journey home. Like Cincinnatus, he planned to live out his days as a gentleman farmer—but his retirement didn't last long.

The Electoral College unanimously elected Washington president in 1789, and he took the oath of office on the balcony of Federal Hall in New York. In his first inaugural address, Washington said in all humility, "I was summoned by my Country, whose voice I can never hear but with veneration and love."[24]

As president, he avoided the trappings of European royalty, insisting on an unpretentious title still in use today: "Mr. President." When Congress approved a salary for the position, Washington refused it. The congressional delegation convinced him to take the money to avoid suggesting that public service was only for the wealthy.[25] Washington's decision to serve only two terms was so influential that all of his successors obeyed the unofficial term limit until Franklin D. Roosevelt broke tradition in 1940. In fact, most of the customs and traditions we associate with the presidency originated with Washington. He invented the office.

In *George Washington's Leadership Lessons*, James Rees, the executive director of Mount Vernon, offers this assessment of Washington's character:

> *One of the most admirable aspects of Washington's character was his sense of*

humility, his self-effacement, his respectful deference to others. He was quick to decline credit and quicker to assign credit to others. He was often vocal about his personally perceived shortcomings and genuinely modest when receiving praise. . . .

Washington truly believed that if a leader selflessly gave everything he had to his country, the people would recognize this sacrifice and act accordingly. They would support him in his efforts without being asked. To promote oneself, or to advertise one's talents, Washington felt, would be crass and ungentlemanly.

This is not to say that Washington lacked confidence—nothing could be further from the truth. But he was seldom cocky or arrogant like so many leaders and high-profile people today.

Washington was, in a word, gracious. [26]

Humility was one of the central pillars of Washington's character. The greater his fame, the greater his humility. His effectiveness as a leader and his success as president were rooted in this rare quality called humility. History's greatest leaders all had it.

Most important of all, Washington's humility, so clearly demonstrated in his refusal to be made king, shaped the future of America.

HUMILITY THROUGH THE AGES

Humility has always been a key factor in the success of high-achieving people.

The Hebrew leader Moses, who stood up to Pharaoh and led his people out of Egypt, was (according to the Bible, in Numbers 12:3) "a very humble man, more humble than anyone else on the face of the earth." When God commissioned him to lead his people out of slavery, Moses protested, "Pardon your servant, Lord. I have never been eloquent, neither in the past nor since you have spoken to your servant. I am slow of speech and tongue" (Exodus 4:10). Though he felt unqualified, historians estimate that he led as many as two million men, women, and children to freedom.

The ancient Greeks prized humility and feared the consequences of excessive pride, which they called *hybris*, from which our English word *hubris* is derived. The Greeks believed that arrogance would cause them to be punished by their vengeful gods. The ancient Romans, however, despised humility and prized arrogance, much as our narcissistic culture does today.

The Chinese philosopher Lao-Tzu, who lived in the sixth century BC, had much to say about the value of humility in leadership and success. Here are a few of his precepts:

> *The sage puts himself last, and yet is first; abandons himself, and yet is preserved. Is it not through his having no selfishness?*

Thereby he preserves self-interest intact.

He that humbles himself shall be preserved entire. He who is self-exalting does not stand high.

I have three precious things that I hold fast and prize, namely: Compassion, economy, and humility. Being compassionate I can be brave; being economical, I can be liberal [generous], and being humble, I can become the chief of men. [27]

A leader is best when people barely know that he exists, not so good when people obey and acclaim him, worst when they despise him. Fail to honor people, they fail to honor you. But of a good leader, who talks little, when his work is done, his aims fulfilled, they will all say, "We did this ourselves." [28]

Who is the greatest example of humility in history? Most would say Jesus of Nazareth. Many years ago, an American minister, Dr. James Allan Francis, wrote an essay called "One Solitary Life," in which he noted that the founder of the Christian faith—which now numbers almost 2.5 billion adherents—was born in obscure circumstances, never owned a home, never traveled more than two hundred miles from the town where He was born, never went to college, never wrote a book, never held public office or ruled a nation—

yet He impacted more human lives than all armies, navies, parliaments, and kings put together. Another prominent minister, Dr. Andrew Murray, wrote that the life of Jesus of Nazareth was marked by one "chief characteristic—the root and essence of all his character." What is that single attribute? Murray says, "His humility."[29]

The call to humility runs throughout the teachings of Jesus. "Blessed are the poor in spirit, for theirs is the kingdom of heaven" (Matthew 5:3). "Take my yoke upon you and learn from me, for I am gentle and humble in heart, and you will find rest for your souls" (Matthew 11:29). "For all those who exalt themselves will be humbled, and those who humble themselves will be exalted" (Luke 14:11).

Theologian and philosopher Augustine of Hippo (354–430) compared living a life of greatness to constructing a great building: "Thou wishest to be great, begin from the least. Thou art thinking to construct some mighty fabric in height; first think of the foundation of humility. And how great soever a mass of building one may wish and design to place above it, the greater the building is to be, the deeper does he dig the foundation."[30]

Down through the ages, humble people have quietly but profoundly changed the course of history and the destiny of nations. The humble will inherit the earth, but they are already shaping it.

A Victory over Ego

Abraham Lincoln was raised in poverty and received very little formal education. In fact, as historian Alexander McClure observed, "In all, Lincoln's 'schooling' did not amount to a year's time, but he was a constant student outside of the schoolhouse. He read all the books he could borrow, and it was his chief delight during the day to lie under the shade of some tree, or at night in front of an open fireplace, reading and studying."[31]

One of the few books Lincoln owned was one he made himself. He borrowed a copy of the printed book, wrote out all the information with pen and paper, then hand-stitched the binding. Lincoln used the book, which contained a table of weights and measures, for learning arithmetic (or "ciphering").

In preparing for his first presidential campaign, Abraham Lincoln wrote a short autobiography. While most presidential candidates would pad their résumés with honors and achievements, both real and imagined, Lincoln's bio was a masterpiece of humble understatement. It began:

> *I was born February 12, 1809, in Hardin*
> *County, Kentucky. My parents were*
> *both born in Virginia of undistinguished*
> *families. . . . My mother, who died in my*
> *tenth year, was of a family of the name of*
> *Hanks. . . . My father. . .grew up literally*

without education. He removed from
Kentucky to what is now Spencer County,
Indiana, in my eighth year. We reached
our new home about the same time the
state came into the Union. It was a wild
region with many bears and other wild
animals still in the woods. There I grew
up. . . .

When I came of age I did not know
much. Still somehow, I could read, write,
and cipher. . . But that was all. I have not
been to school since. The little advance I
now have upon this store of education I
have picked up from time to time under
the pressure of necessity.[32]

There has never been a more self-effacing autobiography ever written. The "little advance" he had on his meager education included teaching himself the law by reading books—and he studied law while serving four terms in the Illinois state legislature. He was admitted to the bar in 1836.

Lincoln married Mary Todd in 1842 and won election to the US House of Representatives in 1847. He served a single term, then retired from politics in disgust. He hated the insincerity and greed of politicians who called themselves "public servants" while they were only in politics to serve themselves. "I was losing interest in politics," he later said, "when the repeal of the Missouri Compromise aroused me again."[33]

Passed in 1820, the Missouri Compromise prohibited the expansion of slavery into the western territories. It was repealed by the Kansas-Nebraska Act of 1854, which permitted slaveholding in new territories west of the Mississippi. Lincoln—a fierce opponent of slavery—was so angered by this betrayal that he returned to political life. In 1856, explorer John C. Frémont was the Republican Party's first presidential candidate; Lincoln ran for vice president. The Frémont-Lincoln ticket lost to Democrat James Buchanan.

In March 1857, the Supreme Court issued the infamous Dred Scott decision, which held that African-Americans were not citizens and had no rights. The Dred Scott decision was intended to settle the slavery question by making slavery permanent. Instead, the decision inflamed passions and put the nation on the path to civil war. The following year, Lincoln delivered his "House Divided" speech, saying, "A house divided against itself cannot stand. I believe this government cannot endure permanently half slave and half free. . . . It will become all one thing, or all the other."[34]

In 1860, Lincoln ran for president and won. On April 12, 1861, five weeks into his presidency, Confederate guns fired on Fort Sumter. The Civil War had begun.

Wartime brought out the best in Lincoln, especially his humility. Lincoln saw himself as a servant of the people and the Constitution. It never occurred to him to expect others to serve him. Once, during the Civil War, a White House servant went into the basement to fetch some supplies—and was startled to find President Lincoln sitting on a bench, shining his boots.

"Mr. President," the servant said, "why are you shining your own boots?"

Lincoln looked up in surprise. "Whose boots should I be shining?"

President Lincoln had great respect for his best generals—but they didn't always respect him. One general in particular treated President Lincoln with arrogance and contempt: General George B. McClellan. During the early days of the war, Lincoln admired McClellan's skill in training and organizing his troops. McClellan had served with distinction during the Mexican-American War and had also been a successful railroad executive.

So Lincoln endured the arrogance of General McClellan. Instead of summoning McClellan to the White House, Lincoln would go to McClellan's house to discuss strategy. The general would make the president wait while he dealt with trivial matters. McClellan's poor treatment of President Lincoln was even noted in newspaper stories. Yet Lincoln humbly endured the abuse, saying, "I will hold McClellan's horse, if he will only bring us success."

Ultimately, McClellan didn't bring the Union Army

success. Though a brilliant organizer, he was a disaster on the battlefield. Lincoln ultimately sacked McClellan, and the infuriated general ran unsuccessfully against Lincoln in the 1864 election.

President Lincoln's humble forbearance extended not only to generals, but even to captains. During an inspection tour of Fort Stevens, at the northern approach to Washington, Lincoln's tour guide was young Captain Oliver Wendell Holmes Jr. (who would later be appointed to the Supreme Court by Theodore Roosevelt).

Through a gap in the wall, Captain Holmes pointed out the location of the enemy. Instead of peering through the gap, Lincoln, wearing his stovepipe hat, raised his head above the wall for a better view. Instantly, the Confederate lines erupted in gunfire.

Holmes shouted, "Get down, you fool!" and threw President Lincoln on the ground. Then the horrified captain realized he had physically assaulted the president of the United States. He was sure he had just destroyed his career—and might even face court-martial.

Lincoln picked himself up, brushed himself off, and continued with the inspection. At the end of the tour, the president said, "Captain Holmes, I'm glad to see that you know how to talk to a civilian." Not another word was said about the matter.[35]

President Lincoln personally visited the hospitals to encourage the wounded. In late 1864, during the Siege of Petersburg, Lincoln visited the Union headquarters in City Point, Virginia. Dr. Jerome Walker, the hospital administrator, guided the president around the hospital wards. Mr. Lincoln offered a word of comfort to each soldier.

Pausing at one ward, Dr. Walker said, "No need to go in there. They're only rebels."

"You mean *Confederates*," Mr. Lincoln said. "I'd like to meet them."

So Dr. Walker took Lincoln to meet the wounded Confederates. The president treated them as if they were his own men, shaking their hands and asking about their families.

Years later, Dr. Walker said he never again referred to Confederate soldiers as "rebels," and he never forgot President Lincoln's act of humble service to the wounded soldiers of both North and South.[36]

President Lincoln was also a humble servant to children. He was delighted whenever children came to the White House. Once, during a Saturday afternoon reception, three young girls wandered in from the neighborhood. They were shabbily dressed and had probably walked into the White House out of curiosity (in those days, the White House was truly "the people's house," not the presidential fortress it is today). President Lincoln beckoned to them and said, "Little girls, are you going to pass by me without shaking hands?" Then he crouched to their level and chatted with them. Witnesses were moved by the president's humble grace.

We see the true depths of Lincoln's humility in his relationship with his secretary of war, Edwin Stanton. Years earlier, Lincoln and Stanton had served on the same legal team together. Stanton hated Lincoln, calling him a "low, cunning clown," a "gorilla," and a man of "painful imbecility."

After Lincoln's first choice as secretary of war resigned, Lincoln invited Stanton to the White House for a talk. Stanton was unaware that the visit was actually a job interview. Near the end of their chat, Lincoln said, "I called you here to offer you the portfolio of War." Stanton thought Lincoln was joking, but the president went on: "I need the best counsellors around me. I have every confidence in your judgment."

Stanton took the job and began reforming the War Department. Lincoln visited the War Office daily, and Stanton was often surly and abrasive toward the president. But Lincoln, knowing that Stanton had restored public trust to the War Department, never doubted that he had chosen the right man.

On one occasion, Congressman Lovejoy from Illinois approached President Lincoln with some ideas for the war effort. Lincoln said, "Explain your ideas to the secretary of war."

So Congressman Lovejoy explained his ideas to Stanton, but the secretary of war was unimpressed. "Did Lincoln send you to me with these ideas?"

"He did, sir."

"Then he is a fool."

Congressman Lovejoy returned to the White House and reported the conversation to the president. Lincoln asked, "Did Stanton say I was a fool?"

"He did, sir."

"Well," Lincoln said, "if Stanton said I was a fool, then I must be one, for he is nearly always right, and generally says what he means. I will slip over and see him."

In time, Stanton softened his opinion of Lincoln, and the two men became good friends. In early April 1865, news reached Washington that, after a nine-month siege by Union forces, General Robert E. Lee and the Confederate government had abandoned the Confederate capital city of Richmond, Virginia. Hearing the news, President Lincoln and Secretary of War Stanton embraced each other.

The president decided to go to Richmond himself. Stanton, fearing for Lincoln's life, begged him to "consider whether you want to expose the nation to the consequence of any disaster to yourself."

Lincoln promised, "I will take care of myself."

So Admiral David D. Porter took President Lincoln up the James River to Richmond aboard the steamer USS *Malvern*. Along with Lincoln and the admiral were Lincoln's twelve-year-old son, Tad, several aides, and an escort of ten or twelve sailors. The *Malvern* did not get far before it was stopped by a line of barriers placed in the river by the Confederates. So Lincoln and his party transferred to a shallow-draft barge, which had to be rowed by the sailors.

Lincoln found it amusing that, after beginning his journey on a powerful steamship, he had to accept a more humble means of transportation. He told Admiral Porter a story. "Admiral," he said, "this brings to mind a fellow who once came to me to ask for an appointment as minister abroad. Finding he could not get that, he came down to some more modest position. Finally he asked to be made a tide-waiter. When he saw that he could not get that, he asked me for an old pair of trousers. . . . It is well to be humble."[37]

When the barge landed, Lincoln stepped off and walked the streets of Richmond, holding Tad's hand. The sailors escorted him closely, nervously checking every window for an assassin. The only people in the streets were emancipated slaves. When a few of them recognized President Lincoln, shouts went up.

"Glory to God," said one. "Glory! Glory! Glory!"

"I know I am free," said another, "for I have seen Father Abraham!"

One freed slave fell on his knees before Lincoln, who said, "Don't kneel to me. That is not right. You must kneel to God only, and thank Him for the liberty you will enjoy hereafter."[38]

Lincoln did not go to Richmond as a conqueror. He went as a humble servant and a healer. It was a two-mile walk from the riverbank to the Confederate Executive Mansion, where Jefferson Davis had presided over the Confederacy. As one of Lincoln's contemporaries observed, Lincoln walked quietly up the street "as the humble citizen President of the United States."[39]

Arriving at the mansion, Lincoln was met at the door by Jefferson Davis's housekeeper, Mary O'Melia, who had stayed behind after Davis fled. She greeted Lincoln cordially and showed him into the library, where the Confederate leader had received generals and dignitaries. Lincoln sat in the chair behind Davis's desk and looked around the library. Then he said softly, "I wonder if I could get a glass of water."

A few minutes later, Major General Godfrey Weitzel arrived. It was Weitzel who had claimed Richmond for the Union, and he was eager to deal harshly with the rebels and teach them a lesson. He asked President Lincoln what sort of measures he should use against the surrendered townspeople. Lincoln gently replied, "If I were in your place, I would let them up easy."[40]

General Robert E. Lee surrendered his army to General U. S. Grant on April 9, 1865, officially ending the Civil War. Five days later, President Lincoln performed his last official acts as president. He pardoned a Union soldier who was to be executed for desertion ("I think this boy can do us more good above ground than underground," he said). And he repatriated a Confederate prisoner who had taken the oath of allegiance to the United States.

That evening, President and Mrs. Lincoln attended

a play at Ford's Theater. Lincoln preferred the plays of Shakespeare, but he attended this play, *Our American Cousin*, as a favor to his wife. At a little after 10:00 p.m., John Wilkes Booth entered the president's box, pointed a derringer behind the president's left ear, and fired one shot at point-blank range. President Lincoln slumped in his chair, mortally wounded.

The wounded president lingered through the night at the Peterson House across the street. Grief-stricken, Edwin Stanton kept vigil, and at one point declared, "There lies the most perfect ruler of men who ever lived."

Lincoln died at 7:22 a.m. on April 15, 1865. For days afterward, Edwin Stanton would visit Lincoln's eldest son, Robert. He wouldn't say a word. He'd just sit beside Robert and weep.[41] Once Lincoln's bitterest foe, Stanton became his closest friend. He was won over by the great humility of Abraham Lincoln.

Writing in the *Psychology Today* blog, Dr. Russell Razzaque said, "Like few leaders the world has known, Lincoln proved that any leader's first and greatest victory is always that over his own ego."[42] The key to Lincoln's greatness was his deep and abiding humility.

HUMBLE RESISTANCE

Mohandas Karamchand Gandhi was born in 1869 in western India. He led a successful movement to liberate India from British colonial rule. His only weapons: a humble spirit and nonviolent civil disobedience. His example inspired other leaders of nonviolent change, including Dr. Martin Luther King Jr. and Nelson Mandela. He is often referred to as "Mahatma," a Sanskrit title that means "Great Soul."

If Gandhi had been a corporation, his brand would have been "Humility." He once said, "I claim to be a simple individual liable to err like any other fellow mortal. I own, however, that I have humility enough to confess my errors and to retrace my steps." And, "It is unwise to be too sure of one's own wisdom. It is healthy to be reminded that the strongest might weaken and the wisest might err."[43]

On one occasion, when Gandhi was a young man, he ran to catch a moving train as it pulled out of the station. He jumped aboard, climbed the steps, then tripped—and one of his shoes slipped off and bounced away along the track. Without hesitation, Gandhi yanked off the other shoe and tossed it toward the lost shoe.

A fellow passenger asked, "Why did you throw your shoe away?"

"The poor man who finds the one," Gandhi said, "will now have two shoes to wear."

Gandhi studied law in England at the Inner Temple, one of the four Inns of Court for English barristers. In those days, Gandhi was worldly and full of youthful arrogance. Novelist George Orwell observed, "Gandhi started out with the normal ambitions of a young Indian student. . . . He wore a top-hat, took dancing lessons, studied French and Latin, went up the Eiffel Tower, and even tried to learn the violin—all this with the idea of assimilating European civilization as thoroughly as possible."[44]

In time, Gandhi discovered the power of deep humility, and he humbly, self-effacingly, shook the foundations of the British Empire. At age twenty-four, he accepted a position as an attorney in Pretoria, South Africa. He had only planned to stay a year in South Africa, but he ultimately stayed twenty-one years. He saw the oppression of Hindu Indians who had immigrated to South Africa as low-paid, unskilled workers. He experienced racism and discrimination.

On one occasion, Gandhi was forced out of the first-class rail compartment he had paid for so that a European passenger could have his compartment. Railway employees told Gandhi he had to ride in the baggage car at the end of the train because he was a "colored" man. When Gandhi protested that he had a first-class ticket, the railway officials put him off the train in the middle of nowhere—stranded with a useless first-class ticket in his hand.[45]

Another time, when Gandhi traveled by stagecoach from Charlestown to Johannesburg, the foul-tempered driver made him ride outside on the coach box instead of inside with the white passengers. At first, Gandhi swallowed his pride and rode on the coach box. But at one stop, the driver continued to bully and insult Gandhi, using racial epithets. Finally, Gandhi raised his fists—and the driver gave him a thrashing. The driver might have killed Gandhi if the other passengers hadn't begged him to stop.[46]

Incidents like these shaped Gandhi's conscience. He began working to empower his Indian countrymen in South Africa and established the Natal Indian Congress to advocate for civil rights. For his efforts, he was vilified, pelted with rocks, and beaten and narrowly escaped being lynched.

Gandhi was deeply influenced by the writings of the Russian novelist Leo Tolstoy, who based his philosophy on the teachings of Jesus of Nazareth, especially the Sermon on the Mount. In 1910, Gandhi cofounded a colony called Tolstoy Farm, outside of Johannesburg. Gandhi and his fellow Tolstoyans lived simple lives, practicing vegetarianism, pacifism, and the avoidance of alcohol, tobacco, and sexual sin. They based their lives on five principles taken from the Sermon on the Mount: love your enemies; do not be angry; do not resist an evil person but turn the other cheek; do not lust; and do not swear an oath.

During this time, Gandhi formulated his ideas of nonviolent resistance—a methodology he called *Satyagraha*, meaning "devotion to the Truth." He taught his fellow Indians in South Africa these principles and urged them to nonviolently defy the racist laws of South Africa. As a result, many nonresisting Indians were flogged, beaten, imprisoned, and killed. Yet the Indian community believed in Gandhi and followed his teachings.

Ultimately, the government's mistreatment of nonresisting protesters troubled the conscience of South African whites. It was hard for the Europeans to see peaceful protesters flogged and beaten. Finally, South African leader Jan Christiaan Smuts agreed to sign the Smuts-Gandhi Settlement of 1914, which guaranteed Indians their civil rights. Gandhi proved that the principles of humble, nonviolent resistance could speak truth to power and bring the oppressors to the bargaining table. His belief was vindicated.

Gandhi returned to India in 1915, to organize the peasants and laborers into a resistance force against the British Empire. He was elected head of the Indian National Congress in 1921 and worked tirelessly for Indian self-rule. The same year, Gandhi adopted the humble loincloth as his trademark. The loincloth was made from homespun khadi cloth, signifying Gandhi's identification with the poor. The symbolism of the loincloth elevated him as a "Great Soul," a Mahatma.[47]

The humble loincloth shocked the conscience of the English people, because it made Gandhi appear naked and uncivilized. Gandhi even wore the loincloth during his audience with King George V at Buckingham Palace. When a reporter asked if Gandhi thought he was properly dressed to appear before the king, Gandhi replied, "Do not worry about my clothes. The king wears enough clothes for both of us."

People often came to the Mahatma for help and advice. One woman brought her small daughter to

Gandhi, asking him to tell her not to eat candy. "The candy is bad for her teeth," the mother said. "My daughter respects you, and she will obey you."

Gandhi said, "Come back in three weeks. When you return, I will see what I can do." So the woman took her daughter in tow and left.

Three weeks later, the woman and her daughter returned. Gandhi set the girl on his knee. "Don't eat candy, child," Gandhi said. "It is bad for your teeth."

The little girl nodded and promised to avoid sweets. Then the girl and her mother left.

Several of Gandhi's friends said, "Did you know that the woman and her child had to walk for hours to see you? Why didn't you give the child that simple advice three weeks ago at their first visit?"

"Three weeks ago," Gandhi said, "I did not know if I could stop eating candy. Since their first visit, I have avoided all sweets. I could not give the child advice unless I knew I could practice it myself."[48]

The British government frequently imprisoned Gandhi. During one of his prison stays, Gandhi invented a portable spinning wheel. That spinning wheel became another Gandhi trademark. He urged the people of India to make their own hand-spun cloth instead of buying cloth from Great Britain—another form of nonviolent resistance.

If you look at the national flag of India, you'll see a blue twenty-four-spoke wheel in the middle of the flag's white center stripe—Gandhi's spinning wheel.

By law, every Indian flag must be manufactured from cloth that was hand-spun on a spinning wheel. Symbols are powerful, and Gandhi's symbol was one of humble resistance to foreign rule.

Another symbolic protest that helped end British rule in India was the Salt March. British taxes on salt were a source of resentment in India. It was against the law for anyone to go to the seashore and harvest sea salt without paying a tax to Great Britain.

On March 12, 1930, Gandhi began his trek from Ahmedabad to the seacoast village of Dandi, a journey on foot of twenty-four days. Arriving at the shore, Gandhi humbly yet defiantly began harvesting salt. He and his followers continued the anti-salt tax resistance for weeks. The British government arrested Gandhi and more than sixty thousand Indians—an overreaction that Gandhi counted on. By arresting peaceful demonstrators for the "crime" of harvesting their own salt, the British government made itself look oppressive and unreasonable.

One year after the Salt March began, Britain freed its political prisoners. Britain also agreed to negotiations with Gandhi regarding Indian independence. The British later violated their agreement and refused to negotiate in good faith. Soon after Gandhi returned from the failed talks in England, the British colonial police arrested him once more.

Two years after the end of World War II, Great Britain finally granted independence to India—but not as Gandhi had wanted. He had envisioned a great nation in which Hindus and Muslims would live together in peace. Britain partitioned India into two nations, Hindu India and Muslim Pakistan. As a result, many Hindus, Sikhs, and Muslims in the border regions were caught in a religious war. Half a million people died in riots.

Gandhi had led the Indian people to independence. But because of the partitioning of the nation, Gandhi believed he had failed.

On the evening of January 30, 1948, when India had been independent for less than six months, Gandhi walked through a garden in New Delhi, accompanied by followers and family members. A Hindu nationalist stepped forward, pointed a pistol at Gandhi's chest, and fired three shots at point-blank range. Gandhi cried out, "O God!"—not an oath, but a prayer. He died at the age of seventy-eight.

George Orwell observed that Gandhi was a brilliant man who could have achieved anything in life. "Inside the saint, or near-saint," he wrote, "there was a very shrewd, able person who could, if he had chosen, have been a brilliant success" in business or politics.[49] Instead, Gandhi chose the humble life of a servant. He stooped to make his own salt. He wore a loincloth of homespun threads. He was a humble man who defied an empire—and won.

Great leaders are always humble leaders—confident, yes; passionate about their mission, yes; persistent and unyielding, yes; but always humble, never self-seeking, never arrogant. The character of America was shaped by the humility of its first president, George Washington—the Cincinnatus of the West, the man who refused to be king. The character of America was refined in the fire of the Civil War by the humble emancipator, Abraham Lincoln. The empire of Great Britain was brought to its knees by "the Great Soul" who spun his own cloth and gathered salt at the seashore.

From the time of Moses to the present day, while kings and generals have worshipped at the altar of power, the hinges of history have turned again and again on the words and deeds of a humble few. While arrogant power has redrawn the map of the world countless times, only humility has produced enduring change. Only humility can found a great nation, emancipate the slaves, hold a war-torn nation together, and expel a foreign oppressor without firing a shot.

Next, let's see how humility continues to be a success factor in the business world today.

3

Humility as a Business Asset

While it takes confidence to push an idea into the marketplace, it's humility that prevents it from turning into arrogance, the idiot cousin of the confident businessperson.
—Branding strategist Erika Napoletano

I arrived in Chicago in the fall of 1969 as the newly named general manager of the Chicago Bulls. I was twenty-nine years old, and though I had confidence in my abilities, I was somewhat intimidated by the eight high-powered businessmen who formed the owner-ship group of the Bulls. Seven of the owners lived in Chicago, and the eighth lived in Dallas, Texas. His name was Lamar Hunt.

Now, I had known Lamar Hunt by reputation for years. He was the founder and owner of the Kansas City Chiefs, the principal founder of the American Football League, and a major promoter of professional basketball, football, tennis, soccer, and ice hockey. In 1966, he proposed that the AFL-NFL championship game be called the Super Bowl—and the NFL made the name official with Super Bowl III in January 1969. Knowing Mr. Hunt's wealth, power, and reputation, the thought of meeting him face-to-face made me a bit weak in the knees.

Soon after I came on board, Mr. Hunt flew to

Chicago for an owners' meeting, and I met him for the first time. He was not at all what I expected. He was soft-spoken, self-effacing, and extraordinarily humble. He didn't treat me as a hireling but as a respected colleague, and he immediately put me at ease. We had a great relationship throughout my time in Chicago.

Mr. Hunt lived a simple, humble lifestyle. He flew coach, wore off-the-rack suits, and drove an old Chevy. As sportswriter Frank Luksa observed in Hunt's ESPN obituary in December 2006, "His manner was cloned from mild-mannered, bespectacled Clark Kent, Superman in disguise. Hunt's persona was quiet-spoken, polite and humble, as flashy as a quarterback sneak. . . . His only extravagance was investing in sports."[50]

One year, the Kansas City Chiefs prepared a press guide, and the publicity department showed it to Mr. Hunt for his approval. He saw that the press guide listed him as the owner of the Chiefs. "I'd rather you not list me as the owner," he said. "That sounds too boastful. List me simply as 'president.' I'm a lot more comfortable with that."

Lamar Hunt was a man of great accomplishments, great significance, and great prominence in the history of American sports. The sports world would look very different today if not for the impact of this one man. Yet he was also a man of deep humility, and I learned a lot about the importance of humility from this great businessman. As the Chiefs' head coach Herm

Edwards said after Lamar Hunt's passing, "He lived his whole life to make a difference, not just to make a living. We can learn something from that. He's very humble, maybe the most humble [man] I've ever been around. In today's world, that's something that you marvel at."[51]

In many ways, Mr. Hunt reminded me of another team owner I had worked for—Mr. R. E. Littlejohn, co-owner of the Spartanburg Phillies minor league baseball team. Mr. Littlejohn was an impressive personality—not because he was flashy or flamboyant, but because he was so amazingly humble. He was a man of wealth, having made his fortune in the petroleum transportation business—yet he was the furthest thing from being a "big shot" as you could imagine.

Mr. Littlejohn was always kind and encouraging to me, and I only saw him angry once—when he leaped to the defense of a radio sports announcer who had been mistreated by the station. I had never met anyone like Mr. Littlejohn before, and I spent a lot of time trying to figure out what made him unique and unforgettable. I now know it was his humility—but I didn't realize it then.

Mr. Littlejohn's humility was undoubtedly connected to his deep Christian beliefs. He candidly said that he tried to model his life after Jesus, though he never tried to push his faith on me or anyone else. I assumed he was simply born with a humble personality and that there was nothing about the man that I could imitate or assimilate. I was wrong.

One day, I said to Mr. Littlejohn, "I think Jesus must have been a lot like you."

I meant it as a compliment—but Mr. Littlejohn was horrified and embarrassed by my statement. He implored me never to say such a thing again. So great was his humility that he even rejected comparisons to the man he consciously emulated.

Mr. Littlejohn became my close friend and mentor, and he continued to impact my life for years after I left Spartanburg. Whenever I had a problem to solve or a major decision to make, I would call Mr. Littlejohn and seek his humble wisdom.

Another business leader who has been a role model of humility to me is Rich DeVos, the cofounder of Amway (Alticor) and owner of the Orlando Magic. *Forbes* estimates his net worth at more than $6 billion— but you'd never guess it to meet him. Whenever he is invited to speak, and his hosts give him a flowery introduction, Rich steps up to the microphone and quite humbly says, "Hello, I'm Rich DeVos, and I'm just a sinner saved by grace."

Looking back over my years in sports management, I am amazed to realize that so many of the owners I have worked for have been great role models of humility. If you want to find some oversized egos, there are plenty to choose from in the business world and the sports world. Yet the most successful leaders I've known have usually been people of deep humility.

That's no coincidence. There's a cause-and-effect relationship between humility and success. Humility is a business asset—perhaps the most important asset you could own.

Egos Anonymous

In August 2015, Turing Pharmaceuticals bought the manufacturing and marketing license for the drug Daraprim from California-based Impax Laboratories. The antiparasitic drug is used to treat and prevent malaria and also to treat potentially fatal *Toxoplasma gondii* infections in unborn babies and patients with HIV or cancer. Upon acquiring the license, Turing's CEO, Martin Shkreli, restricted the distribution and raised the price of Daraprim from $13.50 per tablet to $750 per tablet—an increase of 5,556 percent. The pills cost about a dollar apiece to manufacture, and since Turing purchased the rights to an existing product, the company spent nothing on research and development. Soon after the price hike, the news media began calling Shkreli "the most hated man in America."

On December 17, 2015, the FBI arrested Shkreli—but the charges had nothing to do with pharmaceutical price gouging. Instead, the thirty-two-year-old entrepreneur was accused of illegally using assets from one company to pay off the debts of another company, and bilking investors. Brooklyn US Attorney Robert Capers said, "Shkreli essentially ran his company like a Ponzi scheme where he used each subsequent company to pay off defrauded investors from the prior company."[52] He was freed on a $5 million bond.

If a Mount Rushmore of Gigantic Egos is ever carved, Shkreli will probably be on it, elbowing Donald Trump aside to slip in between Madonna and Kanye West. Shkreli frequently tweets on Twitter and live-streams on YouTube, boasting of his wealth, his lifestyle of lavish excess, and his taste in music. Unlike your average hardworking corporate CEO, Shkreli seems to spend most of his time sitting at home, playing online computer games, and live-streaming such pearls of wisdom as, "I feel so cool. I've got so much swag."[53] He spent millions to buy the only copy of a Wu-Tang Clan album that the rap group made as a publicity stunt. When presidential candidate Hillary Clinton urged him to cut the cost of Daraprim, his only reply was a tweet that read, "LOL."

In February 2016, Shkreli was summoned to Capitol Hill to testify at a House hearing on drug pricing. On advice of counsel, he refused to answer any questions—yet he did smirk at the questioners. Sometimes he pointedly looked away from his questioners and smiled for the news photographers in the room. One congressman remarked, "I don't think I've ever seen the committee treated with such contempt," while another chastised Shkreli for his "childish, smart-aleck-ish smirks."[54] After mugging and stonewalling his way through the hearing, he tweeted: "Hard to accept that these imbeciles represent the people in our government."[55]

As I write these words, Martin Shkreli has been forced out of the biotechnology firm Retrophin (which he cofounded), forced out of Turing (which he founded), sued by Retrophin for $65 million, indicted for securities fraud, and taken the Fifth before a House committee. The day of his arrest, his $45 million E*Trade account, which he posted to make bail, plummeted in value to somewhere below the $5 million bail amount.[56] If convicted, he faces up to twenty years in federal prison and could be banned from working in the securities industry.[57]

Surrounded by a sea of hatred and righteous indignation, Martin Shkreli didn't have the sense to at least put on an act of humility. Instead, he poked his thumb in the eye of the public and the government that is indicting him. Every time he opens his mouth or sends out a tweet, he makes more new enemies.

"His fatal mistake was his arrogance and snarkiness," said Richard Levick of Levick Strategic Communications. "In a crisis, you're judged by how you do in your worst moment. I would've admonished him to think before he spoke."[58] Martin Shkreli seems arrogantly committed to digging an ever-deeper hole for himself.

Would a twenty-year prison stretch teach this arrogant punk a lesson in humility? Probably not. But it might at least wipe the smirk off his face.

Management experts Ken Blanchard and Scott

Blanchard (Ken's son) conduct "Egos Anonymous" sessions for top executives in big companies. Though the name "Egos Anonymous" is tongue in cheek, the work Ken and Scott do is serious business. They gather the execs in a circle, as in a recovery group meeting. Then they talk about the times their arrogance has hindered them from dealing with business problems, peers, clients, or employees. Executives open up and confess their ego-driven mistakes. Then Ken and Scott help them develop humility-based strategies to overcome their ego-driven habits and behaviors.

"The ego is one of the biggest barriers to people working together effectively," Ken and Scott wrote in *Fast Company*. "When people get caught up in their egos, it erodes their effectiveness. The combination of false pride and self-doubt created by an overactive ego gives people a distorted image of their own importance.... That's a deadly combination in today's business environment, where organizations need people to work together collaboratively to meet the ever increasing expectations of customers."[59]

Arrogance is an expensive liability on your balance sheet. Humility is an asset.

Humility pays.

The Way of Humility

Silicon Valley, the technological epicenter of California, came into existence on August 23, 1937. That was the day two recently graduated electronics engineers decided to start their own company. Their names: Bill Hewlett and Dave Packard.

As Bill and Dave discussed the kind of company they wanted to build, they developed a vision for a company that would invent and market original products. The notes of their discussion have been preserved as a kind of founding document for the company known as Hewlett-Packard. Near the end of those notes comes this statement: "The question of what to manufacture was postponed to a later date."

I think that's a fascinating statement. When Milton Hershey founded the Hershey Chocolate Company in 1893, he knew that his product was going to be chocolate candy. When Henry Ford founded the Ford Motor Company in 1903, he knew that his product was going to be automobiles. When Steve Jobs and Steve Wozniak founded Apple Computer, Inc., in 1976, they knew they were going to build and sell personal computers. But when Hewlett and Packard founded their company, they didn't know what their product would be. They didn't set out to build a certain kind of product. They set out to build a certain kind of *company*.

Once they had founded their company, Hewlett and Packard considered making audio amplifiers for phonographs, electronic shock machines that would jiggle people to help them lose weight, control boxes for air-conditioning systems, electronic boundary markers for bowling alleys, and much more. They actually built working prototypes for a number of products for which they had no buyers, and predictably, those products failed.

Finally, they invented the Model 200A audio oscillator. What does an audio oscillator do? It electronically produces a pitch-perfect sound at a specific frequency, and it can be used to test and maintain radios, telephones, and stereophonic sound equipment. Why was it called "Model 200A"? Because Hewlett and Packard wanted to give the impression the company had been around awhile and had already produced 199 previous products.

They wrote letters to potential buyers—and the first company to show any interest in the audio oscillator was The Walt Disney Company. At the time, Disney was working on an ambitious motion picture called *Fantasia*, which would employ multiple audio channels, each of which needed to be precisely calibrated. The Disney Company asked Hewlett-Packard to make some special modifications to the Model 200A, and the modified version became known as the Model 200B. Disney purchased eight units of Hewlett-Packard's first successful product.

The most important Hewlett-Packard invention was not a product but a culture—an idea that became known as "The HP Way." The Hewlett-Packard management style simply did not exist before Bill Hewlett and Dave Packard founded their company. Though the values embodied in The HP Way were not written down until years after the company was founded, the corporate culture of Hewlett-Packard was distinct from the beginning. The HP Way is expressed in five statements of principle:

1. We have trust and respect for individuals.
2. We focus on a high level of achievement and contribution.
3. We conduct our business with uncompromising integrity.
4. We achieve our common objectives through teamwork.
5. We encourage flexibility and innovation. [60]

The HP Way was an innovative idea from an innovative company. No other major corporation operated on a set of principles like these. Before Hewlett and Packard built their company, corporations always treated profit as king. But according to the five principles of The HP Way, the company was going to put individuals, contributions to the community, integrity, teamwork, and innovation ahead of profits.

In 1949, Dave Packard received an invitation to join a group of business leaders and financiers in the Bay Area. It was an exclusive club made up of business tycoons. Thirty-seven-year-old Dave Packard sat down in a meeting and listened to the other business leaders talk about ways to extract more profit from workers and customers. As he listened, Dave grew uncomfortable. There was no sense of gratitude to the people who generated those big profits.

Finally, Dave Packard rose to his full six-foot-five-inch height and spoke up. "A company has a greater responsibility than making money for its stockholders," he said. "We have a responsibility to our employees to recognize their dignity as human beings." He added that the workers who helped generate the wealth had a moral right to share in the wealth they produced.

The other executives in the room—all older and wealthier than Dave—looked at him as if he were a bomb-throwing Bolshevik. He could read on their faces that they unanimously regretted having invited him to the meeting. He knew he didn't belong and he never went back.[61]

The HP Way has become part of the lore not only of Hewlett-Packard, but of the entire Silicon Valley community. But many people misunderstand what The HP Way is about. Some think it was a commitment by Bill Hewlett and Dave Packard never to fire anyone—and it's true that HP employees enjoyed almost continual job security, even during tough economic times. But that doesn't mean Bill and Dave were opposed to firing unproductive employees.

In 1970, HP marketing manager Bill Krause (who later became chairman of 3Com) was hospitalized for months following a serious automobile accident. Dave Packard visited Krause at the hospital and told him not to worry about anything except getting well—his job would be waiting for him when he was ready to return. Years later, however, when Bill Krause was in a meeting, explaining to his bosses why his department was underperforming, the same Dave Packard who had been so compassionate to Krause said, "Customer satisfaction second to none is the only acceptable goal. If you cannot lead our organization to achieve that goal, I'm sure we can find someone who can."[62]

Treating employees with compassion was part of The HP Way—but so was customer satisfaction. The HP Way guaranteed that Hewlett-Packard would put individuals ahead of profits—but customers are individuals, too. If HP employees couldn't keep customers happy, those employees would be replaced by someone who could. That, too, was The HP Way.

The Hewlett-Packard business philosophy was demonstrated through a number of innovative employee benefits. HP was one of the first companies in the world to share its profits with its workers through stock options and other profit-sharing premiums. These measures built employee incentive and morale and gave them a sense of ownership and identification with the company. HP also provided scholarships for the children of employees.

Hewlett and Packard practiced what they called the open-door policy. Every employee could go over the heads of middle managers and speak straight to Bill and Dave. Employees were encouraged to call the founders by their first names. This policy, rooted in the essential humility of Bill Hewlett and David Packard, created a family feeling among the employees that produced a huge practical benefit. Union organizers frequently showed up at HP headquarters, seeking to unionize the workers. The unions got nowhere, because everyone at HP was happy with the status quo. Why pay union dues if working conditions, pay, and job security were as good as they could get?

During slow economic times, when HP had to tighten its belt, the company never laid off workers. Instead, Hewlett and Packard would cut back working hours. For example, they might close the plant every other Friday. These occasional unpaid three-day weekends meant a pay cut for employees—and Hewlett and Packard took their pay cuts along with everybody else. No one ever complained about the reduced hours and reduced wages. In fact, morale was so high that Hewlett and Packard had to post guards at the doors to keep employees from entering the plant and working for free.

All of these policies reflect the personal humility of these two corporate leaders, Bill Hewlett and Dave Packard. One longtime HP employee recalled a company lunch he attended shortly after arriving at the Palo Alto headquarters in the early 1970s. "I was running a bit late," Steve Sinn recalled. "I thought I was going to be the last person into the room. Much to my surprise, I turned around and found David Packard standing behind me."

Packard put out his hand and introduced himself, and the two men chatted as the lunch line moved forward. "He was warm and friendly," Sinn said. "It was like talking to an old friend. He asked me a few questions and seemed genuinely interested. I will remember it always."

Only later did Steve Sinn realize that Packard probably did this all the time—waiting for the last person in line, then stepping up to make that person feel welcome and at ease. The iconic position Dave Packard held at HP became obvious as Sinn and Packard stepped through the door into the lunch room. "The group hushed, all heads turned his way," Sinn recalled. "David became the company patriarch at that very moment. . . . It was an amazing transformation. He just was a different person for the group than he was when we were talking one-on-one."[63]

Another longtime HP employee, Fred Schroder, recalled having Dave and his wife, Lu, over for dinner a few times. "Dave loved home cooking and sauerkraut and hated restaurant eating," Schroder said. "He wanted to sit in the kitchen watching our preparations of the meal and entertaining the party." When Schroder's daughter came into the kitchen and asked for help with her math homework, Dave volunteered. "My daughter finished her work quickly with his tutoring," Schroder concluded, "and treasures a picture of that evening till this day."[64]

Bill Hewlett was also known for his humility

and kindness to his employees. Jackie Spinozzi, who worked in the accounting department at HP Labs, recalled attending a company barbecue and standing in line for a grilled hamburger. Next to her in line was Bill Hewlett. When he reached the server, he asked for two burgers—one for himself and one to take back to his secretary. The server, a newly hired young woman who didn't recognize the cofounder, said, "I'm sorry, but they told me I can only serve one hamburger per person."

"Well," Hewlett said, "that's okay."

Spinozzi leaned over to the server and said, "This is Bill Hewlett."

The flustered server looked wide-eyed and offered to give him a second burger.

"Oh, no," Hewlett said, "I'm happy to follow the rules."[65]

In 1967, Bill Hewlett answered his home phone, and heard a boy say, "I'm twelve years old, and I want to build a frequency counter for my school science project. I was wondering if you have any spare parts I could have." How did the boy get Bill Hewlett's home phone number? Easy. Hewlett was in the phone book. Not only did Bill Hewlett give the boy the parts he needed, but that summer, he gave the boy a job on the Hewlett-Packard assembly line, helping to build frequency counters. That young tech wizard could hardly believe he was actually working at Hewlett-Packard. Oh, did I forget to mention the boy's name? It was Steve Jobs.[66]

Bill Hewlett retired from the company in 1987, and Dave Packard retired in 1993. Many observers say the company they founded began to stray off course in the late 1990s and early 2000s as a new generation of leaders began losing sight of The HP Way—the humble core principles that made HP great. Bill Hewlett and Dave Packard put individuals ahead of profit and that's how they achieved greatness.

The HP Way is a formula for organizational humility. It is based on the personalities and principles of two humble guys, Bill Hewlett and Dave Packard. In 1958, Packard prepared a simple document to be distributed at an IIP management convention in Sonoma, California. That document contains eleven pieces of advice, and the first ten of those eleven pieces of advice are simply statements of how to live humbly in a corporate environment. Here is a summary of those eleven pieces of advice:

1. First think of the other person.

2. Reinforce the other person's feeling of importance.

3. Respect the other person's individuality.

4. Offer sincere recognition to those who do well.

5. Eliminate anything negative (avoid criticism and disapproval).

6. Avoid trying to change people.

7. Try to understand the other person.

8. Check your first impression. ("If I don't like this man," Abraham Lincoln once said, "I have to get to know him better.")

9. Be careful in the small details (your smile, tone of voice, eye contact, and other small interactions).

10. Develop a genuine interest in people.

11. Persevere. That's all, persevere! [67]

Dave Packard's eleven rules are simply a prescription for living humbly toward others—putting other people ahead of oneself, ahead of ego and self-importance, ahead of selfish ambition, ahead of profit. These rules are an expression of Dave Packard's personal values.

When Dave and Bill formulated The HP Way, they wanted to build their company on a foundation that was consistent with who they were and what they believed. In the process, they created a formula for organizations that endure. If the organization Hewlett and Packard founded can find its way back to The HP Way, it may again become the dominant industry leader, as in the days when its humble founders were at the helm.

Seven Traits of a Humble Leader

Genuine humility can be as tough as nails when it needs to be. A genuinely humble leader understands the truth of the old adage, "Better a lion leading an army of sheep than a sheep leading an army of lions." Humility isn't about being a sheep. It's about being a shepherd. It's about putting the interests of the customer, the employee, the partner, the stakeholder, and the shareholder ahead of one's own selfish interests.

You can spot a humble business leader by a number

of traits. Here are seven examples of humble leadership traits:

1. *Humble leaders are always learning.* They don't assume they have all the answers. They are humbly curious. They are always reading. They listen to the ideas of people around them, including subordinates. They encourage fresh insights and suggestions from people at all levels, from board members to janitors.

Marie Stempinski, founder of Strategic Communication in St. Petersburg, urges arrogant executives (she calls them "Chief Ego Officers") to make a deliberate effort to build humility into their executive skill set. She writes, "Successful leaders know when to talk and when to listen. They are open to new ideas and new ways of doing things. And they arc open to change if the change makes sense and helps the business or organization grow and prosper."[68]

One way great leaders demonstrate a humble eagerness to learn is by admitting mistakes. Some leaders refuse to admit mistakes, thinking that it will cause their followers to lose respect for them. Nonsense. When a leader makes a mistake, it's usually obvious to everyone. When a leader says, "I was wrong," he or she only acknowledges what everyone else already knows. Subordinates usually have greater respect for leaders who admit mistakes than leaders who pretend to be infallible.

Defensiveness is our default setting. We don't want to admit we are wrong. We bristle when we are criticized—or even when people politely offer a suggestion. The antidote for defensiveness is humility—a humble admission that we don't have all the answers. Humility helps us to avoid ignorance, mistakes, and self-deception. It keeps us on the path to truth.

2. *Humble leaders are servants.* They understand that their success is built on the successful efforts of everyone in the organization, so their first objective is not to make themselves look good but to serve people and help them succeed. A humble leader is willing to set up chairs, make coffee, and mop up spills.

When I was learning the ropes in the sports management business, one of my first mentors was the great baseball executive Bill Veeck. He was responsible for many of the innovations in the game, including putting players' names on uniforms and celebrating home team triumphs with fireworks. In the summer of 1962, I called and told him I wanted to learn from him. He could not have been more kind and welcoming. He was retired, and I visited him at his estate in Easton, Maryland, overlooking Chesapeake Bay.

His autobiography, *Veeck as in Wreck*, had been out for a few months and I brought my copy for him to sign. I expected him to be a loud, brash baseball promoter. Instead, Bill Veeck turned out to be a gentle, humble, soft-spoken man. In fact, when I drove up to his house, he was sitting on the front porch, reading a book of poetry. He was a good listener, and he seemed interested in me and in everything I had to say.

He gave me a lot of priceless advice that day, and over the years that followed. One of the most important words of advice he gave me was, "Take good care of your people." Bill was always available to his players and staff. Whenever he bought a ball club, his first official act was to take his office door off its hinges and put it in storage. Bill Veeck's doorless office was a powerful symbol that he was always available, always ready to listen, and always a humble servant to his players and staff.

Throughout my career in sports, I have tried to emulate Bill Veeck's humble management style. Though my office does have a door on it, that door is rarely closed when I'm at work. I want to be a servant to the people who work with me. I want to be known as a leader who is accessible, a good listener, and genuinely humble.

3. *Humble leaders respect the individual.* That means respecting employees—and customers. It means listening to people, then letting them know that you hear them and you empathize with them. It also means helping them to meet their goals. Respecting the individual can also mean respecting people enough to give them your honest opinion, even if it's not pleasant for you or the other person. When you respect people, you tell them the truth—not to hurt them, but to help them.

4. *Humble leaders surround themselves with smart people.* Arrogant, ego-driven people are essentially insecure. They fear that having bright, capable people around them will somehow diminish them, so they hire people who won't threaten their fragile egos.

Legendary advertising man David Ogilvy, founder of Ogilvy & Mather Worldwide, once returned from a trip to Russia with a number of Russian dolls. At the next meeting of his agency's board of directors, he placed a doll on the table in front of each director, then told them to open the dolls. Inside the doll was another, smaller doll. Inside that was another. Inside that was another.

Finally, each director found a note inside the smallest doll. That note, from Ogilvy himself, read, "If you always hire people who are smaller than you are, we shall become a company of dwarfs. If, on the other hand, you always hire people who are bigger than you are, we shall become a company of giants."[69]

Humble leaders hire people with bigger talent, bigger ideas, and bigger and better ways of doing things. That's why a company led by a humble leader is more likely to become a company of giants.

5. *Humble leaders surrender control.* Arrogant people have a dysfunctional need to control everything. They tend to be demanding and inflexible. But humble leaders are comfortable with a certain amount of ambiguity. Yes, they hold their subordinates

accountable for results—but they empower their sub-ordinates to make decisions about how to achieve those results.

One of the most effective ways to destroy the morale in your organization is to micromanage everybody and everything. Hover over your people, second-guess them, punish them for every mistake, interfere with them at every turn—that kind of micromanagement destroys the effectiveness of your people, and it's a sure sign of an arrogant leader. The arrogant leader says, "Everything has to be done my way. I always know best. No one can do anything as well as I can." The humble leader says, "Use your best judgment. I won't punish you for mistakes—just don't make the same mistake twice. I trust you. I believe in you."

So humbly surrender control—and let your people prove how brilliant you were to hire them.

6. *Humble leaders demonstrate genuine empathy and caring for subordinates.* When players know their coach is truly interested in their best interests, they will run through walls for that coach. When employees know their boss truly wants the best for them, they will arrive early, stay late, and do whatever it takes to make that business a success. Humble leaders inspire loyalty and respect. That's why humble leaders so often succeed where arrogant leaders fail.

7. *Humble leaders treat customers like royalty.* There is a reason why the saying "The customer is always right" has endured. Businesses that treat their customers as

chumps, as sheep to be fleeced, are only in it for the short haul. But businesses that truly listen to their customers and serve their needs are built to last. This is true no matter what business you're in.

If you're in politics, treat your constituents like royalty. If you're an author, treat your readers like royalty. If you're a doctor, treat your patients like royalty. And if you're a sports executive, treat the fans like royalty. This is another lesson I learned from the great Bill Veeck.

Bill always answered his own phone and opened his own mail—and when fans wrote to him, he wrote back. During games, he would roam the ballpark, mingling with the fans. After the games, he stood at the gate and shook hands with people as they left, chatting with them and thanking them for coming. I have modeled my own leadership style after his, and to this day I answer my own phone, answer my mail, visit with the fans in the arena, and shake hands with them as they leave. Bill taught me to treat my customers as royalty, and I've never forgotten that lesson.

THE FORCE OF GRAVITY AND THE POWER OF HUMILITY

One day in March 2015, Dan Price, the young (thirty-one-year-old) CEO of Seattle-based Gravity Payments, took a mountain hike with his friend Valerie. As they hiked, Valerie confided in Price that she faced a $200-a-month rent increase that would severely strain her budget. She was working fifty hours a week and making $40,000 a year at her regular job, while augmenting her income by managing residential properties on the side. She was even thinking of giving up her car to cut expenses, though she couldn't imagine how she could manage residential properties by taking the bus.

As Valerie poured out her tale of woe, Price—who was pulling down a $1.1 million CEO's annual salary—realized that a third of his employees at Gravity Payments were making even less money than Valerie was. He asked himself, were his employees paying the rent out of their 401(k)s, sleeping on friends' couches, or making other painful sacrifices? He knew how hard they worked. Some, he later recalled, "stayed up all night in their pajamas answering phone calls from clients, canceled Friday night dates to help merchants in emergencies and went outside of their job description to make sure the independent businesses we served achieved incredible success." He realized that, for the sake of profit, "I was actively chipping away at the well-being of my team. How was that right?"[70]

On April 13, 2015, one month after his eye-opening hike with Valerie, Dan Price announced a new policy to the 120 people on his team: henceforth, the minimum salary at Gravity Payments would be $70,000 a year. What's more, Price was defraying these new employee costs by cutting his own salary from $1.1 million to $70,000.

The raises would be phased in over three years, with

a minimum of $50,000 in the first year, $60,000 in the second, and $70,000 in the third. Price promises he will accomplish these increases without raising prices, without layoffs, and without cuts to executive pay— except his own. The plan would raise—and in many cases *double*—the pay of some seventy workers.

Dan Price's decision was covered by NBC and *The New York Times*, and the news exploded all over social media. One Yahoo executive was so inspired by Price's example that she quit her job and went to work for Gravity Payments at more than 80 percent less than her Yahoo pay, saying she wanted a job that was meaningful and fun.

Along with all that good press came some harsh media backlash. Rush Limbaugh condemned Dan Price's experiment as "socialism." Others called it a publicity stunt. Two employees resigned, saying that Price's actions were unfair to those who were paid more because they produced more for the company. Dan Price's own brother, Lucas, a partner in the company, filed suit, claiming that Dan had previously accrued "excessive compensation."

Dan Price believes he is building a happier, more motivated workforce, which will pay off in higher productivity, increased sales, and higher client retention rates. As a bonus, the publicity Gravity Payments received sent new client inquiries soaring from the old average of thirty per month to more than two thousand in just two weeks. As a result, the company had to hire more people to handle the increase in business.

In the first few months after the announcement, revenue doubled. Some Gravity clients defected for a reason Dan Price did not foresee: by boosting the salaries of his own workforce, Price inadvertently caused some of his corporate clients to feel the heat from their own employees. Overall, however, Gravity's client retention rate improved after the announcement.

Writing in *Inc.*, financial writer Paul Keegan observed, "Raising your cost of doing business is generally not considered the best way to increase profits and improve market position. Yet. . .Price says establishing a $70,000 minimum wage is a moral imperative, not a business strategy. . . . 'I want the scorecard we have as business leaders to be not about money, but about purpose, impact, and service,' he says. 'I want those to be the things that we judge ourselves on.' "[71]

Now, I'm not suggesting that every business should set a $70,000 minimum salary for its employees. In fact, very few businesses could do that without going broke. Entry-level jobs were never designed to provide a "living wage" for a family breadwinner. Entry-level jobs with entry-level pay scales give young and unskilled workers a chance to enter the workforce even when they have very little to offer an employer.

The point of the Dan Price story is this: Your humility just might be your most important business asset. Your humble willingness to listen and learn, to admit mistakes and change course, to be a servant to others, to respect and care for the employees who work with you, to demonstrate empathy and caring for your subordinates—these are assets that will always contribute to your business success and your bottom line.

How you live out humility in your business life is up to you to decide. The conditions you confront and the decisions you face are not the same as those faced by Dan Price or Bill Hewlett or Dave Packard. Every company, every industry, every leader, every employee, and every individual customer is unique. But people with the grace and humility to listen, learn, grow, care, and respect the people they serve will be able to meet those challenges today, tomorrow, and on into the future.

In the next chapter we will explore strategies for ensuring that our humility is authentic and focused on making a difference in the lives of others.

4

Genuine Humility— or Just an Act?

False modesty can be worse than arrogance.
—English novelist David Mitchell

I never miss the NBA All-Star Weekend. In February 2016, it was held in Toronto, and I took my two oldest sons, Jimmy and Bobby, and my Magic publicity manager, Andrew Herdliska. We were in the lobby of the hotel when I spotted the famous Canadian athlete and Hall of Fame pitcher, Ferguson Jenkins.

Fergie was my teammate for two years with the minor league Miami Marlins, in 1962 and 1963. He went on to a stellar career from 1965 to 1983, pitching for the Philadelphia Phillies, Chicago Cubs, Texas Rangers, and Boston Red Sox. He was the first Canadian to be inducted into the Baseball Hall of Fame and has always been a great friend to me.

So Jimmy, Bobby, Andrew, and I went over to greet Fergie, and he was glad to see us. He looked at my sons, and the first words out of his mouth were, "Your dad was my first catcher in professional baseball—and he was a good one." He went on to praise me and tell them what a great catcher I was—which, of course, I wasn't. But it sure felt good to have a Hall of Famer telling my boys such nice things about their old man.

Genuine humility puts others first, gives credit to other people, and speaks well of other people—even when they don't deserve it. Fergie is a genuinely humble guy.

In January 2011, while I was in the midst of promoting a book about Coach John Wooden, I was diagnosed with multiple myeloma, a cancer of the plasma cells. I announced my cancer battle at a press conference in Orlando and was uplifted and encouraged by the expressions of support I received from across the nation. I sent a copy of my book to golfing legend Arnold Palmer, and within a few days, I received a letter from Arnold, who was treated for prostate cancer in 1997 and lost his wife, Winnie, to ovarian cancer in 1999. He wrote:

> *Pat—*
>
> *I understand you're going through a tough time right now. I wish you all the best with your treatment, and would only give you the same advice that people gave me when I was going through my ordeal: listen to what your doctors advise you and keep a positive attitude. All the best,*
>
> *Arnold Palmer*

Every victory in life begins with optimism and hope—and Arnold's kind note had given me a massive infusion of both. I had the letter framed, and I hung it on the wall of my office. I mentioned that letter to Arnold's best friend, Howdy Giles, and told him that I had gotten the letter framed as a constant reminder.

Well, Howdy told Arnold, and Arnold was genuinely surprised. "I can't believe Pat Williams would frame a letter of mine," he said.

Arnold has no idea what his words of encouragement mean to me. Genuine humility shows kindness to others without even realizing how much that kindness might mean. Arnold Palmer is a genuinely humble guy.

In November 2015, I was making my way home after a speaking engagement in Greenville, North Carolina. I was supposed to change planes in Charlotte, but as the plane made its descent toward Douglas International Airport in Charlotte, I was doubled over with stomach cramps, coughing fits, and a broiling fever. The flight attendants told me I could forget about my connecting flight.

When the plane reached the terminal, a phalanx of first aid technicians put me in a wheelchair, then loaded me into a waiting ambulance and rushed me to the hospital. Word of my illness reached my longtime friend Bobby Jones. Bobby had played for the Philadelphia 76ers when I was the general manager, and he had lived most of his life in Charlotte.

Now, here's the amazing thing: when I arrived at the hospital emergency room, Bobby was already waiting for me. He hadn't come merely to wish me well. He came to stay with me and serve me. He was at my side while I was being admitted, and he stayed with me through the night and all the next day. There wasn't anything Bobby wouldn't do to make me more comfortable.

And I do mean *anything*. At one point, I needed help with bedpan duties. The nurses were unavailable—but a six-foot-nine former NBA star named Bobby Jones was on the job, performing those duties for his old GM. That's humility in action. During his playing days, Bobby was known as one of the most unselfish players in the NBA, but you don't know what "unselfish" really means until a friend humbly helps you with bedpan duties. Bobby Jones is a genuinely humble guy.

Humility must be genuine. If our "humility" is only an act, who is it for? And what good is it?

The Deceitful Appearance of Humility

Michael Keaton gained fame as a comedic actor in films such as *Night Shift*, *Beetlejuice*, and *The Dream Team*, and also distinguished himself in dramas and action films such as *Clean and Sober*, *Batman*, and *Batman Returns*. In 2014, Keaton drew acclaim for his appearance in *Birdman*, directed by Alejandro González Iñárritu. The role earned him a Golden Globe Award and an Oscar nomination, both for Best Actor.

Interviewed in January 2015, a week before the Academy Awards gala, Keaton said he was excited about the nomination. "It feels good," he said. "I'm in a new phase. I don't mean this in an arrogant way but I'm so confident at how good this film is that if everyone said it was the worst thing they'd ever seen, I'd be okay with it. . . . I hate the false humility thing. I hate it as much as the 'look how cool and groovy I am' thing."[72]

How does that statement strike you? Would you rather hear an actor say, "Aw, shucks, folks, I am so undeserving! All this fuss for little ol' me?" Or would you rather hear an actor say, without either arrogance or false humility, "I'm confident that this is a good film"? Between you and me, I think Michael Keaton hit just the right note of humble confidence, without arrogance. There's nothing wrong with taking pride in a job well done—and I'm speaking here of the pride of craftsmanship, not arrogant and egotistical pride.

There is no human trait more attractive than genuine humility. And there are few traits more unappealing than false humility. Jonathan Pearson, pastor of Cornerstone Community Church in Orangeburg, South Carolina, writes: "One of the most prideful things you and I can do is show false humility. False humility is nothing more than pride with a mask. . . . People can see through our disguise."[73]

Why do we so engage in false humility? Often it's because we want the benefits that come with humility without having to give up our pride. In our arrogance, we want people to see us as humble. It really strokes our egos to hear people tell us how modest and sincere we are. Phony humility is the sincerest form of arrogance.

During Easter season 2014, a congresswoman went to an Episcopal church and joined with the bishop in a symbolic ceremony of washing the feet of undocumented immigrants. The custom of serving others by the washing of feet goes back to an incident recorded in the Gospels in which Jesus of Nazareth took a towel and a basin of water and demonstrated His humble servanthood by washing the feet of His disciples. For two thousand years, the towel and the basin have symbolized humility.

So when this congresswoman took part in the foot-washing ceremony, she demonstrated her own humble spirit by this symbolic act of service—or did she? Soon after the church service was over, the congresswoman's official Twitter account sent out a photo showing her washing the feet of two immigrant children.

We have to ask ourselves: How authentic is our act of "humility" if we tweet a photo of our "humility" on social media? The response to the congresswoman's tweet was immediate and scathing, including tweets of "You are such a phony millionaire politician" and "The photo op of all photo ops!"

I choose to withhold judgment and give this congresswoman the benefit of the doubt. I choose to believe that she genuinely wanted to perform a humble act of service and caring to people in need. I certainly have no way of knowing if her motives were self-serving or not. I only know that, at the very least, tweeting about your humility tends to nullify your good works. "Tooting your own horn" makes your act of service seem like false humility.

Genuine humility is quiet, even shy. Humility doesn't announce itself.

One of the most famous lines in Jane Austen's 1813 novel *Pride and Prejudice* is spoken by Mr. Darcy: "Nothing is more deceitful than the appearance of humility." In fact, he adds, false humility is "sometimes an indirect boast."

C. S. Lewis observed that a genuinely humble person would probably not be the kind of person you would even think of as "humble." Lewis describes what a truly humble person would be like:

> *Probably all you will think about him is that he seemed a cheerful, intelligent chap who took a real interest in what you said to him. If you do dislike him it will be because you feel a little envious of anyone who seems to enjoy life so easily. He will not be thinking about humility: he will not be thinking about himself at all.*
>
> *If anyone would like to acquire humility, I can, I think, tell him the first step. The first step is to realize that one is proud. And a biggish step, too. At least, nothing whatever can be done before it. If you think you are not conceited, it means you are very conceited indeed.* [74]

Lewis has presented us with an intriguing paradox: The mere thought, "I am humble," is proof positive that you are arrogant. The moment you think that thought, you cease to be humble. At that very instant, you have become proud of your humility. In fact, if you pray, "God, I thank You for my humility," you are praying an *arrogant* prayer.

Humility must be genuine.

Nobody Act Big, Nobody Act Small

There are many forms of false humility. Some people put on an act of phony humility to impress and manipulate others—*false humility*. Some people are just unassertive doormats who let other people take advantage of them—*false humility*. Some people have a habit of running themselves down and belittling themselves, and what they are really doing is fishing for compliments from other people—*false humility*. Sometimes employees will put on a show of complying with the boss's orders, pretending to be humble, cheerful, and eager to serve, but when the boss isn't looking, they slack off or sabotage the task in some way—*false humility*.

Many of us have a hard time accepting compliments. If someone offers us a word of encouragement or affirmation or praise, we feel we must deflect it. That, too, is false humility. Instead of rejecting compliments, practice saying a simple "thank you" or "you're very kind." Don't let it swell your ego—but don't toss it away, either. Accept it—humbly.

Actor Jim Caviezel has had major roles in such films as *The Thin Red Line*, *The Count of Monte Cristo*, and the CBS crime drama series *Person of Interest*, but he is best known for his role as Jesus in the 2004 film *The Passion of the Christ*. A devout Roman Catholic, Caviezel told an interviewer how he prepared himself mentally and spiritually to portray the ultimate role model of humility. Caviezel knew he couldn't bring a sense of false humility to the role—his humility had to be authentic. And that meant he needed to go deeper into his faith, deeper into his understanding of the humility of Jesus.

"I couldn't become him," Caviezel said. "It was whether he wanted to come into me. I had to dance for him. I had to do the work. I had to get on my knees and pray. . . . Every day I'm trying to be more humble, and how do you do that? I guess, every day, we have mass. Every day, I pray the rosary. That's what I do."[75]

The supreme test of Caviezel's humility came after the film was released. Every successful actor knows the experience of meeting fans who confuse the actor with the role. The problem is compounded when the role is Jesus. Caviezel recalled, "A woman in Mexico wanted me to heal her. But I can't heal anybody. I just put my hand on her and said, 'Thank you for seeing the film.' "[76]

No one is born humble. We are all born self-centered. We quickly learn that other people don't

underlying asset). Soon the company was paying him hundreds of thousands of dollars to advise professional investors about derivatives—and he was just twenty-six years old.

Lewis later wrote a book about his experiences as a Wall Street bond salesman in the late 1980s—*Liar's Poker: Rising Through the Wreckage on Wall Street*. The book sold a million copies and made Michael Lewis a star. "All of a sudden people were telling me I was born to be a writer," he recalled. "This was absurd. Even I could see there was another, truer narrative, with luck as its theme. What were the odds of being seated at that dinner next to that Salomon Brothers lady? Of landing inside the best Wall Street firm from which to write the story of an age? Of landing in the seat with the best view of the business? . . . Of having been let into Princeton in the first place?"[78]

Now, I want to interject at this point that I don't believe in "luck"—unless you are using the word as a synonym for "random chance." I don't believe in having a run of "good luck" or "bad luck" or the notion that a rabbit's foot or a four-leaf clover is a "good luck charm." I do believe in the goodness and grace of divine Providence. And I believe we can improve our odds of success through hard work, focus, careful planning, and perseverance, but I reject the superstitious notion that "Fortune" may sometimes smile on us and bring us "good luck."

When Michael Lewis talks about "luck," I think

he refers to random chance. He's saying that, in spite of all of his hard work as a bond salesman and later as a bestselling author, he attributes much of his success to factors beyond his control, such as being at the right place at the right time. He is humbly saying that his considerable success as an author is largely attributable *not* to his own individual merit, but to *random* factors, which he calls "luck."

His point is that we should not take ourselves and our success too seriously. We should not arrogantly give ourselves too much credit for our achievements. There's an automatic advantage to being born into a middle-class American suburb instead of a remote village in Afghanistan or Ethiopia. None of us can claim to have chosen our parents or our birthplace or the culture and economic climate we were born into. So, no matter how successful we may be, we have every reason to be humble, and no reason to be arrogant.

Replace False Humility with the Real Deal

"Pride makes us artificial," said Thomas Merton, "and humility makes us real." So it stands to reason that if our humility is artificial, it must be *false* humility. We are easily deceived by prideful motives. How can we learn to distinguish between genuine humility and false humility? And how can we learn to cast phony humility out of our lives?

Let me suggest some practical ways we can become more authentically humble as we learn to remove the false masks of humility we hide behind:

1. *Take time to reflect on the person you are—and the person you want to be.* If we are genuinely humble, we are keenly aware of the disparity between who we are and who we aspire to be. We recognize that we have not already arrived, in terms of our character, integrity, and accomplishments. We are works in progress.

We need to remember that it's easy, over time, to become someone we really don't want to be. We see people who are arrogant and self-centered, and we wonder, "How do people get that way? Why would anyone *choose* to be such an obnoxious creep? I never want to be that kind of person." But time passes, you achieve some wealth, some power—and it goes to your head. You start to feel entitled, start to think that maybe you really *are* better than other people. You want to fit in with other wealthy, powerful people. Little by little, without even realizing it, you've changed—and not for the better.

Roderick M. Kramer, a professor of organizational behavior at Stanford, says he has seen people undergo this kind of unconscious transformation again and again. Citing examples like Enron's Kenneth Lay or Tyco's Dennis Kozlowski, Kramer observes that many "corner-office titans" have been on a path to "sky's the limit" success only to become engulfed in scandal brought on by arrogance. "One moment they are masters of their domain," he writes. "The next they are on the pavement looking up, wondering where it all went wrong."

In his classroom, Kramer warns students of the seductiveness of power and the fact that wealth, fame, and success can change people before they realize it, in ways they don't expect. He adds, "When I ask respondents to explain why they think the process of experiencing great success will not change them in any fundamental way, they typically say something along the lines of, 'Because I know what kind of person I am'. . . . It is as if in finding success they will become merely bigger and better versions of what they are now. They can't even imagine that they could ever fall from grace. And that, of course, guarantees that some of them will."[79]

In order to guard against a fall from grace, we need to step back, look at the big picture of our lives, and reflect on who we are—and who we truly want to be. We need to think about how we treat the people around us, from our closest family members to the people who mow our lawns and fill our water glasses at the restaurant. Have we improved with age and achievement—or have we become the kind of people we used to detest?

Don't fall prey to arrogance. Take time to reflect. Be very careful and deliberate in choosing the person you will be.

2. *Ask a few trusted friends to be brutally honest with you.* Enlist the help of people who will level with you for your own good. One of the best role models

of this principle is bestselling author Jerry Jenkins. I first met Jerry in 1969, when I was general manager of the Chicago Bulls. In those days, he was a young feature writer for a newspaper in suburban Chicago. He wanted to do a story about me, and though I couldn't imagine why his readers would be interested in a young NBA executive, I agreed to the interview.

Sometime later, Jerry contacted me and said, "If you'd be willing, I'd like to work with you on a book."

"A book about what?"

"About your life. Your autobiography."

As soon as I stopped laughing, I said, "You've got to be kidding. I'm twenty-nine years old. Shouldn't I *live* my life before I write a book about it?"

"If I can convince a publisher to make an offer, would you say yes?"

"Jerry, if you can interest a publisher, which I doubt, then I'd be honored to work with you."

Six months later, Jerry came to me and said, "I've got a publisher."

So we wrote my autobiography, *The Gingerbread Man*, and it was published in the fall of 1974. It was the first of ten books Jerry and I worked on together. We were in the middle of our eleventh collaboration when Jerry called and said, "Pat, I'm sorry, but I'm going to have to bail out of this book we're writing. I'm working on another project, and it has taken over my life. I just don't have time to write the next book with you."

The other project Jerry was writing was a novel

called *Left Behind*, in collaboration with Tim LaHaye. That book became an enormous success, and the first in a series of bestsellers.

Jerry is still a good friend, and I can testify that success hasn't changed him. He remains as humble, down-to-earth, and unpretentious as when I first met him in 1969. I once asked him, "Jerry, the *Left Behind* series is a publishing phenomenon. How has success affected you?"

"Well, there was a period there where I was receiving a check for more than a million dollars every month. It gave me a new understanding of young athletes who start earning crazy amounts of money and are not equipped to handle it."

"So how do *you* handle it?"

"Pat," he said, "I've got a group of men around me, and they meet with me, pray with me, and hold me accountable. I've told them, 'If I ever start acting like a jerk, please slap me upside the head.' And believe me, they will."

We all need people in our lives who will hold up a mirror and show us who we truly are so we won't be walking around with the moral equivalent of spinach in our teeth. Truth is a powerful antidote to self-deception and false humility. If you always have people in your life who will tell you the truth for your own good, and if you humbly need their wise counsel, they will save you from a multitude of self-inflicted wounds.

3. *Immediately and humbly admit your faults and failures.* In other words, apologize without delay. Anyone who tries to achieve anything is bound to make mistakes. The greater your goals, the bigger your potential blunders. Our natural tendency is to deny our failings and shortcomings. We don't like to admit that we've messed up. We prefer to protect our pride and our egos.

In May 2013, the then-mayor of Toronto (who has since died of cancer) was accused in the press of being a crack cocaine addict. He initially responded with denial: "I do not use crack cocaine, nor am I an addict of crack cocaine."

In November, as evidence continued to mount that the mayor was a drug abuser, he told the press, "Yes, I have smoked crack cocaine. Probably in one of my drunken stupors." When the media and the public clamored for his resignation, the mayor offered what is famously called a "non-apology apology." He said, "You know what, I made mistakes, I drank too much, I smoked some crack sometimes. What can I say? I made a mistake, I'm human."[80]

The what-can-I-say-I'm-human non-apology is actually a form of arrogant defiance disguised as humility. Admitting to being "human" is not much of an admission. It's just another way of saying, "Don't you dare judge me. I'm human and so are you. I make mistakes and so do you, and I make no apologies. So what are you going to do about it?"

The mayor's continued rationalizing of his irrational behavior eventually became too much for Torontoites to tolerate. The mayor was forced to step down. Everyone can see through the arrogance of a "non-apology apology." People are rightly offended when their elected officials behave self-righteously instead of humbly. But when a leader genuinely admits failings and errors of judgment, people are quick to forgive.

In April 1961, the recently inaugurated President John F. Kennedy approved a plan to send a CIA-sponsored paramilitary group to invade Castro's Cuba at a place called the Bay of Pigs. The invasion failed, and the Cuban Army killed or captured the US-sponsored troops. The incident was a huge embarrassment for the United States. The failed attack solidified Castro's power in Cuba and strengthened Castro's relationship with the Soviet Union. After the failed invasion, President Kennedy delivered a speech before the American Society of Newspaper Editors in which he accepted responsibility for the failure. He spoke of the "useful lessons" to be learned, and added, "We intend to profit from this lesson."[81]

After his apology, President Kennedy's approval ratings soared in spite of the foreign policy disaster. The American people are quick to forgive a leader who humbly admits his mistakes and apologizes for them.

In 1986, another foreign-policy debacle—the Iran-Contra Scandal—threatened to engulf the Reagan administration. The scandal arose from a CIA plan to funnel aid to anti-Communist Contra rebels in Nicaragua, a violation of the Boland Amendment. The Iran-Contra scheme came to light on November 3, 1986; ten days later, President Reagan gave a televised address to the nation from the Oval Office and announced an independent investigation commission. The commission completed its work in about three months. On March 4, 1987, President Reagan again addressed the nation:

> *I take full responsibility for my own actions and for those of my administration. As angry as I may be about activities undertaken without my knowledge, I am still accountable for those activities. As disappointed as I may be in some who served me, I'm still the one who must answer to the American people for this behavior. And as personally distasteful as I find secret bank accounts and diverted funds—well, as the Navy would say, this happened on my watch. . . .*
>
> *What began as a strategic opening to Iran deteriorated, in its implementation, into trading arms for hostages. This runs counter to my own beliefs, to administration policy, and to the original strategy we had in mind. There are reasons why it happened, but no*

excuses. . . . As President, I cannot escape responsibility. [82]

With that apology, Ronald Reagan put the Iran-Contra scandal in the rearview mirror. The scandal clouded the Reagan presidency for just four months, from November 3, 1986, to March 4, 1987, and then it was over. R. W. Apple Jr., of *The New York Times*—no friend of the Reagan administration—applauded the president's apology:

> *President Reagan spoke to the American people tonight in a spirit of contrition that has not been heard from the White House in a quarter century. . . . Not since John F. Kennedy took the blame for the catastrophic Bay of Pigs invasion in 1961 has any President so openly confessed error. . . .*
>
> *The President, an inveterate optimist, conceded that the report of his special review board, headed by former Senator John G. Tower of Texas, was "well-stocked with criticisms;" he said he accepted them all, without exception, and called them "honest and convincing". . . .*
>
> *He drew the moral of the story in simple words, applicable to any household—the kind of thing a parent*

says to a child after a major setback.

"What should happen when you make a mistake is this," he said. "You take your knocks, you learn your lessons and then you move on. That's the healthiest way to deal with a problem. You learn. You put things in perspective. You pull your energies together. You change."[82]

The Reagan apology was an act of genuine humility, nothing false about it. It was specific and detailed, and the president took the onus of blame upon himself.

If President Reagan had not apologized, the achievements of his final two years in office might never have happened. The "Tear Down This Wall" speech at the Brandenburg Gate, the Washington and Moscow summits with Mikhail Gorbachev (which reduced nuclear stockpiles in both countries), and the end of the Cold War all came about *after* Mr. Reagan's historic apology. Without that apology, those final two years would have been consumed by controversy.

If you want to recover from a moral failure or a lapse in judgment, the key is to apologize fully, specifically, and humbly. Don't try to get away with a non-apology apology. Be sincere. Take your lumps. Learn your lessons—and learn from our greatest leaders like Kennedy and Reagan.

4. *Be honestly humble and humbly honest.* Don't inflate your résumé—but don't deflate it either. It's perfectly wise and acceptable to own your achievements and state your qualifications. Just don't brag or take more credit than you've earned.

There's never any need for false modesty. If someone asks if you possess certain skills or experience, answer honestly but humbly: "Yes, I've had experience at that," or, "Yes, I've had success with that." Honest self-assessment and self-affirmation sounds much more humble than phony humility.

False modesty tends to break down authentic humility because it becomes hard to know where your real humility leaves off and your phony humility begins. You become so accustomed to devaluing your own talent, accomplishments, and self-worth that you actually lose confidence in yourself. You stop speaking up, stop advocating for what you believe, stop pursuing your own goals. In short, you start believing your own self-deprecating falsehoods.

In situations where you need to market yourself, such as a sales pitch or job interview, don't brag but don't undersell yourself. Avoid flamboyance or exaggeration, but offer a solid and persuasive description of the traits, abilities, and accomplishments you bring to the table. Whenever possible, offer outside perspectives—online reviews, newspaper write-ups, letters of recommendation—to substantiate your claims from an objective point of view.

Don't hide your weaknesses, but don't hide your strengths, either.

Genuine humility is the best policy. False modesty comes from ego and pride. As Canadian humorist Eric Nicol observed, "I am keenly aware of the need to avoid false modesty. Which, like false teeth, can make you talk funny."[84]

THE HUMILITY OF THE TREE-SHAKER

Nelson Mandela was born in 1918 in the village of Mvezo in South Africa. His patrilineal great-grandfather was Ngubengcuka, a legendary king of the Thembu people. Nelson's clan name was Madiba, and his parents named him Rolihlahla, a Xhosa word meaning "Tree-Shaker," one who shakes things up and brings change.

After Nelson's father died, his mother took him to the Great Place, the Thembu palace at Mqhekezweni, to live as a ward of Chief Jongintaba Dalindyebo. The chief and his wife raised Nelson as their own son and sent him to school at a Methodist mission school near the palace.[85]

Nelson attended tribal meetings in the courtyard of the Great Place, where he saw his foster father lead in a spirit of humility. Chief Jongintaba would convene the meeting—then he would listen to the concerns of the tribesmen, withholding comment until the end of the meeting. "Everyone was heard," Mandela later recalled, "chief and subject, warrior and medicine man, shopkeeper and farmer, landowner and laborer."[86] Even when people complained or criticized the chief, he never interrupted or defended himself. He humbly responded to the complaints. He used his tribal authority to serve his people, never to serve himself.

Chief Jongintaba's example of humble leadership had a big influence on Nelson Mandela's life. Nelson grew up wanting to be the kind of leader who helped people. When he attended university, friends tried to recruit him into the African National Congress. Though he believed in many of the aims of the ANC, he rejected the organization because of its ties to Marxism.

During the early 1940s, Mandela worked as a law clerk in Johannesburg, working alongside people of many races—black Africans, Indians, Europeans, Jews, and people of mixed race. They all got along as equals. Many of his friends were involved with the Communist Party, and he gradually became attracted to radicalism, though he always rejected violence as a political solution.

He studied law at the University of Witwatersrand, where a friend finally convinced him to join the ANC. Because of his radical activities, his studies suffered. In 1949, after Mandela failed his final year at Witwatersrand for the third time, the school expelled him. Mandela began reading Marx, Engels, and Lenin—yet he was also influenced by Mohandas Gandhi and his principles of nonviolent resistance, which contrasted with the violent tactics of the Communists.

Steve Bloom, son of South African anti-apartheid activist Harry Bloom, tells of an incident from the 1950s that illustrates the essential humility of Nelson Mandela. Once, while walking in Johannesburg, Mandela saw a white woman standing beside her car, which had broken down. Mandela offered to take a look and see if he could fix it. He opened the hood, fiddled with the engine, and the car started right up.

The woman reached into her purse, pulled out some money, and offered it to him—but Mandela wouldn't take it. "Oh, no," he said. "I'm only too happy to help."

Amazed, the woman said, "Why would you, a black man, help a white woman if you didn't want money?"

Mandela seemed puzzled by the question. "Because," he said simply, "you are stranded by the side of the road."

In 1961, after the court issued a warrant for his arrest, Mandela spent two months hiding out in the one-room Johannesberg apartment of Wolfie Kodesh, a Jewish immigrant from Eastern Europe who was committed to the black struggle for freedom. Kodesh later recalled that he and Mandela had an argument about who would sleep where. Kodesh wanted Mandela to sleep in his bed, but Mandela insisted on sleeping in a fold-away cot (or "camp stretcher").

Kodesh recalled, "I said to him, 'Well, I'll sleep on the camp stretcher. You sleep on the bed because you are six foot something, I am five foot something. So the stretcher is just right for me.' No, he wasn't going to have that. He hadn't come there to put me out, and we had a bit of a talk about that and. . .it was arranged, and I would sleep on the bed."[87]

In August 1962, police arrested Mandela. He actually welcomed the arrest, believing a trial would give him a platform from which to make his case for equal rights. The trial began on November 26, 1963, and lasted for many months. Mandela was charged with sabotage and collaborating with Communists to overthrow the government. Mandela represented himself and called no witnesses in his defense.

On April 20, 1964, Mandela delivered his famous "I Am Prepared to Die" speech, concluding with these words: "I have cherished the ideal of a democratic and free society in which all persons will live together in harmony and with equal opportunities. It is an ideal which I hope to live for and to see realized. But, My Lord, if it needs be, it is an ideal for which I am prepared to die." [88]

Nelson Mandela's speech was officially censored by the South African government, but excerpts leaked out and appeared in newspapers around the world. The United Nations and the World Peace Council called for Mandela's release, but on June 12, 1964, the court found Mandela guilty on all charges and condemned him to life in prison with hard labor.

He was sent to Robben Island, the nation's harshest

prison, where he remained for eighteen years. He slept on a straw mat in a cell that measured eight by seven feet. He worked in the limestone quarry, where the glare of sunlight on white stone permanently damaged his eyes.

In August 1989, F. W. de Klerk became president of South Africa. He believed that apartheid had to end and the government had to grant equality to black Africans—or the nation would be plunged into a race war. In February 1990, the de Klerk government released Nelson Mandela from prison.

In a speech from Cape Town's City Hall, Mandela said, "I stand here before you not as a prophet but as a humble servant of you, the people. Your tireless and heroic sacrifices have made it possible for me to be here today. I therefore place the remaining years of my life in your hands." Mandela then asked his fellow South Africans, both black and white, to join him in a commitment to reconciliation and racial harmony.[89]

In 1994, Mandela electrified the nation by announcing that he was running for president of South Africa. Rick Stengel, a *Time* magazine writer who worked with Mandela on his autobiography, *Long Walk to Freedom*, recalled a plane flight Mandela took during his presidential campaign.

"Mandela got on a tiny propeller plane to fly down to the killing fields of Natal and give a speech to his Zulu supporters," Stengel said. "When the plane was twenty minutes from landing, one of its engines failed.

Some on the plane began to panic. The only thing that calmed them was looking at Mandela, who quietly read his newspaper as if he were a commuter on his morning train to the office. . . .

"The pilot managed to land the plane safely. When Mandela and I got in the backseat of his bulletproof BMW that would take us to the rally, he turned to me and said, 'Man, I was terrified up there!' "[90] The moral of this story: a humble leader serves his people by maintaining a calm, confident demeanor even in a crisis.

During the presidential campaign, F. W. de Klerk represented the National Party while Nelson Mandela represented the African National Congress. The two men met in a televised debate that ended with Mandela taking the initiative to reach out and shake de Klerk's hand. It was a visible symbol of Nelson Mandela's dream of a racially united South Africa. Soon afterward, Nelson Mandela became South Africa's first black African president. With that election, apartheid ended and South Africa became a multiracial democracy. It was the first time the black African majority had achieved political power without bloodshed.

As president, Nelson Mandela conducted himself with typical humility. He visited his boyhood village, greeted the townspeople, and even took time to settle tribal disputes. He lived simply and humbly, donating a third of his income to the Nelson Mandela Children's Fund.

Jessie Duarte, President Mandela's personal assistant, recalled, "He always made his own bed, no matter where we traveled. I remember we were in Shanghai, in a very fancy hotel, and the Chinese hospitality requires that the person who cleans your room and provides you with your food, does exactly that. If you do it for yourself, it could even be regarded as an insult. . . . I tried to say to him, 'Please don't make your own bed, because there's this custom here.' And he said, 'Call them, bring them to me.'"

So Duarte asked the hotel manager to bring the cleaning staff to President Mandela's room. Once the staff was assembled in Mandela's room, President Mandela explained through an interpreter that he always made his own bed, and they should not feel insulted. His explanation was humble and gracious, and the cleaning ladies were moved and grateful that he was considerate of their feelings.

There was nothing false or affected about Nelson Mandela's humility. It was authentic, through and through. "He didn't ever want to hurt people's feelings," Duarte concluded. "He never really cared about what great big people think of him, but he did care about what small people thought of him."[91]

Nelson Mandela retired from politics in 1999 after one term as president. His people would have gladly made him president for life, but at age eighty-one, Mandela was tired. He had accomplished his dream. So he retired to the role of a humble elder statesman.

On December 5, 2013, at age ninety-five, Nelson Mandela died at his home in Johannesburg, surrounded by his family. The nation, and the world, mourned the passing of a truly humble leader. He had earned the name he'd received in childhood. He was Rolihlahla, the Tree-Shaker, the one who shook the nation and brought change to the world through his gentle, humble leadership.

White South African novelist André Brink was a friend and confidant of Nelson Mandela. After Mandela became president, Brink visited him at Genadendal, the presidential residence in Cape Town. Over tea, the two men talked about how South Africa had once been an outcast country, sanctioned and condemned by the nations of the world. Now South Africa was transformed, a moral and political role model for the world. Brink kidded Mandela, saying, "That is all your fault."

Mandela waved off the compliment and replied that if he had influenced South Africa for the better, it was because the people and the nation were ready to embrace change. But Brink knew that South Africa could not have changed without a humble leader to guide the nation on its perilous journey "between white fears and black hopes."

"It is part of Mandela's charm," Brink concluded, "that he can be humble without a hint of false modesty."[92]

Humility without false modesty was the key to

Nelson Mandela's amazing success in ending apartheid and transforming South Africa without bloodshed. What are your "impossible" goals, your "unattainable" dreams? Learn the lesson of the Tree-Shaker. Be humble without false modesty, and see where your journey takes you.

5

Humble Confidence—
Striking the Right Balance

Talent is God-given. Be humble. Fame is man-given.
Be thankful. Conceit is self-given. Be careful.
—Coach John Wooden

Symphony conductor Lorin Maazel was eight years old in 1938 when he first raised a baton and conducted an orchestra. At age eleven, he guest-conducted the NBC Symphony Orchestra for a live radio broadcast. From the 1950s until the year of his passing, 2014, he led numerous orchestras in concert halls across Europe and America.

In his early career, Maazel was often described as a demanding, forbidding, and even terrifying taskmaster in rehearsals. But he mellowed significantly in his later years. In a 2003 interview with *USA Today*, Lorin Maazel explained the change in his character during his mature years.

"When you're young," Maazel replied, "you can become pretty arrogant. I learned gradually to be ever more humble. At the same time, not having self-confidence and undermining faith in yourself is very bad. Some performers are very self-destructive. They don't do their best because they're always tearing their performances apart, always feeling inadequate.

Others are totally in love with themselves, incredibly arrogant. You need to find a good balance between self-confidence and humility."[93]

Lorin Maazel put his finger on the paradox of success: In order to achieve great goals, we need confidence and humility in perfect harmony. We need to have confidence in our abilities, trusting that, with hard work, focus, and clear goals, we *can* and *will* succeed. Yet we must never let our confidence turn into arrogance. Alongside our confidence, we need a humble and unpretentious sense of ourselves as fallible human beings with much to learn.

We need confident humility. Or if you prefer, humble confidence.

One person I've met who strikes that perfect balance is evangelist Billy Graham. I first met him when I was in college. He has a striking, charismatic presence, piercing blue eyes, and an unmistakable personal magnetism. He is one of the most recognized people on the planet, yet he's also the most humble and self-effacing man I've ever met.

His youngest daughter, Ruth, once appeared on my local radio show. I asked her to describe her father. "My daddy knows who he is," she said, "a flawed human being. In his mind, he's still just a farm boy from Charlotte, North Carolina."

Management researchers Jim Collins and Jerry I. Porras, authors of *Good to Great*, spent five years studying the traits of executives whose companies achieved greatness, according to a number of objective benchmarks. Collins and Porras found that executives who exemplified "a paradoxical combination of personal humility plus professional will" achieved what they called "Level 5 Leadership."

They tell the story of Darwin E. Smith who, in 1971, became the CEO of a faltering paper company, Kimberly-Clark. Smith had previously been an unknown in-house attorney, and one of the directors told him he wasn't qualified to be the CEO of a major corporation. Yet Smith went on to have a two-decade career as CEO. During that time, he transformed Kimberly-Clark into the leading consumer paper products company in the world, outperforming such giant corporations as Coca-Cola and General Electric.

Few people have ever heard of Darwin E. Smith. Why? Unlike many CEOs, Smith had no interest in the limelight. As Collins explained, "Smith is a classic example of a Level 5 leader—an individual who blends extreme personal humility with intense professional will. According to our five-year research study, executives who possess this paradoxical combination of traits are catalysts for the statistically rare event of transforming a good company into a great one."[94]

Any individual who possesses that paradoxical combination of humility and confidence has laid the foundation for transforming a good career into a great career, a good life into a great life. To succeed, we need confident humility. We need humble confidence.

A Dissenting Opinion

What if I'm wrong?

What if humility *isn't* the secret ingredient to success after all? What if all truly great leaders are actually *narcissists*—people who exhibit the very opposite of *humility*: excessive self-love, self-admiration, and arrogance?

This is not an idle question. While researching this book, I came across an article in a business journal that seems to contradict everything I'm telling you. In an early 2000 issue of *Harvard Business Review*, psychoanalyst Michael Maccoby introduced a notion he called "productive narcissism." He wrote:

> *Most people think of narcissists in a primarily negative way. After all, Freud named the type after the mythical figure Narcissus, who died because of his pathological preoccupation with himself.*
>
> *Yet narcissism can be extraordinarily useful—even necessary. . . . [Productive narcissists] are gifted and creative strategists who see the big picture and find meaning in the risky challenge of changing the world and leaving behind a legacy. Indeed, one reason we look to productive narcissists in times of great transition is that they have the audacity to push through the massive*

transformations that society periodically
undertakes. Productive narcissists are not
only risk takers willing to get the job done
but also charmers who can convert the
masses with their rhetoric. [95]

In 2003, Maccoby expanded his article into a book, *The Productive Narcissist.* In it, he claims that the self-centered traits of narcissism are useful and even essential to successful leadership. Why does Michael Maccoby sing the praises of narcissism? His claims and mine are diametrically opposed. Who's right?

Part of the problem is semantic. Maccoby defines many terms—including *narcissist* and *narcissism*—differently from the rest of us. Near the beginning of his book, he states, "I want to bring about a radical new definition of the term [*narcissism*]."[96] He thinks it's unfortunate that most people see a narcissist as a "vain, self-centered egomaniac." He claims that what he calls "productive narcissists" actually have many positive qualities. Productive narcissists, Maccoby says, are (1) visionaries who reject the status quo and who believe they can change the world, (2) skilled communicators who attract followers with their vision, and (3) bold risk takers who get the job done.[97]

But the qualities that Michael Maccoby ascribes to "productive narcissists" are simply leadership traits. In my 1996 book *The Magic of Teamwork,* I introduced a concept I call "The Seven Sides of Leadership," which are:

1. Vision
2. Communication Skills
3. People Skills
4. Character
5. Competence
6. Boldness
7. A Serving Heart

These seven qualities are learnable skills. The more skilled a leader becomes in each of these seven dimensions of leadership, the more effective and successful a leader he or she is likely to be. Michael Maccoby lists three of these leadership traits—vision, communication skills, and boldness—as traits of a so-called "productive narcissist." I believe Maccoby's "radical new definition" of a narcissist is misleading and unnecessary. He's not describing a *narcissist*. He's describing a *leader*.

In fact, the most productive, effective, and successful leader of all is one who has the Seventh Side of leadership, which I call "A Serving Heart." In other words, the best and most successful leaders are the exact *opposite* of narcissists—they are humble servants.

MACCOBY VERSUS LINCOLN

Who does Michael Maccoby cite as an example of "productive narcissism"? Brace yourself. He picks Abraham Lincoln. That's right, Maccoby calls Lincoln—the quintessential icon of humility and a serving heart—a narcissist. How does Maccoby support such a claim?

Maccoby offers, as Exhibit A, Lincoln's love of books, which he calls an "early form of rebellion" by the young Abraham Lincoln. In other words, Lincoln didn't read out of a love for reading. He read as a way of defying his father, who put no stock in "book learning." Maccoby explains:

> *[Lincoln's] cousin said: "Lincoln was lazy—a very lazy man—He was always reading—scribbling—writing—Ciphering—writing Poetry." A neighbor and former boss said: "Abe was awful lazy: he worked for me—was always reading & thinking—used to get mad at him." His friends and family saw him as a rebel who didn't listen to his father or boss; I see him as a narcissist who rejected the social demands in favor of his own vision, one that wasn't reinforced or encouraged by his peers.* [98]

The notion that Lincoln's love of "book learning" somehow points to narcissism strains credulity. More likely, Lincoln simply *enjoyed* reading. When Lincoln was fourteen, a cousin named John Hanks came to live with the Lincolns for a while. Hanks later described young Lincoln's daily routine after they finished their chores: "He would go to the cupboard, snatch a piece of corn-bread, take down a book, sit down on a chair, cock his legs up as high as his head, and read. . . . Abe read constantly when he had an opportunity."[99]

Exhibit A—Lincoln's love of books—is less than persuasive. Does Maccoby offer an Exhibit B to support the claim that Lincoln was a narcissist? Yes, he does: Lincoln's ambition. Maccoby explains:

> *Lincoln's contemporaries never considered him shy or humble; they thought he was extremely ambitious at an early age, a big personality and presence, outspoken, a charismatic speaker and performer, and aggressive when it came to his career. According to Lincoln's law partner, William Herndon, "His ambition was a little engine that knew no rest." Lincoln even pushed the limit of legality during the 1858 senatorial race against Stephen Douglas by suggesting that his campaign sway voters at the polls with "a true man, of the 'detective' class. . .among them in disguise, who could, at the nick of time, control their votes." Hardly the act of a shy and retiring personality.* [100]

Michael Maccoby seems to confuse terms and definitions. Humility is not being "shy and retiring," nor does humility mean that a person lacks ambition. Humble people can make big, ambitious plans, can be outspoken and charismatic, and can be assertive in pursuit of their goals. And arrogant people can be completely devoid of ambition, believing that they are entitled to have success handed to them without effort.

Humility is not a personality trait, like being shy and introverted. Humility is an *attitude choice* that even ambitious and extroverted people can make. Humility is the absence of arrogance, the choice to maintain a modest and realistic estimate of one's own importance.

Maccoby also quotes Lincoln out of context, creating the false impression that Lincoln tried to win his 1858 senatorial race by cheating. On October 20, 1858, Abraham Lincoln wrote a letter to Norman Buel Judd, a member of the Illinois Senate, expressing his concern that the Douglas campaign was plotting to import false voters into closely contested districts to stuff the ballot box. Lincoln suggested that whenever his campaign people discovered a group of false voters, they should plant a "detective" among them to get them to switch allegiance. "Think this over," Lincoln concluded. "It would be a great thing, when this trick is attempted upon us, to have the saddle come up on the other horse." Lincoln's suggestion was not an attempt to "sway voters at the polls" but a defensive strategy to prevent cheating by an unscrupulous opponent.[101]

Exhibit B is just as unconvincing as Exhibit A.

Where, then, is Maccoby's evidence that Lincoln was a narcissist? That's it! That's his case—Lincoln's love of books and his ambition. And Maccoby ignores the mountain of evidence for Lincoln's genuine humility.

Lincoln biographer James Baird McClure collected many accounts by Lincoln's contemporaries that illustrate his genuine humility. Judge A. G. W. Carter described a speech Lincoln gave in Cincinnati in 1859:

> *I full remember the modest and humble beginning of his great speech:*
>
> *"Fellow-citizens," said he, in a very sincere manner and plain tone of voice, "this is the first time I ever undertook to speak to the people inhabiting so large a city. . . . I hope I will be excused for any errors or blunders that I may make before so large a meeting."*
>
> *This was truly a humble beginning, and the very simplicity and homespun manner and method of his exordium commanded at once the attention of the people.* [102]

Judge Carter also recalls a conversation he had with Governor Thomas Corwin of Ohio. Corwin told Carter of a conversation he had with Lincoln that demonstrated "the thorough simplicity, humility, and modesty of the character of Abraham Lincoln." Judge Carter recalled the Lincoln-Corwin dialogue:

"Well, Mr. Lincoln," said Mr. Corwin, "the people begin seriously to talk about you as a candidate for the Presidency. . . ."

Lincoln—"Oh, the talk is not serious at all. . . ."

Corwin—"But it is serious, and as the convention of the Republicans will assemble early next year. . .they will perhaps nominate you."

Lincoln—"What! nominate me, when there are such great men as Seward and Chase? . . . I don't encourage the idea, and shall not encourage the idea, for I have no ambition to be president. That never entered my head. Indeed, Mr. Corwin, I do not think I am fit to be President of these United States. I have not the requisite ability. I am not competent to fill the Presidency. . . . Now, I'll tell you what—I am willing to run for Vice-President, if the convention will nominate me for that, and with a little study of Cushing's or Jefferson's Manual I might acquire enough knowledge to sit in the chair of the Vice-President and preside over the deliberations of the Senate. You know it does not require a great genius to do that. . . . I know that I am not fit to be President, and I know that the people know that, too."[103]

Those are hardly the words of a narcissist. A true narcissist loves to hear himself talk. Though Lincoln could certainly hold his own against a long-winded opponent (each of the seven Lincoln-Douglas debates lasted three hours or more), Lincoln didn't have a narcissist's fondness for the sound of his own voice. In an age of flowery oratory, his speeches were simple, plainspoken, and frequently short.

Lincoln delivered his first political speech at age twenty-three while running for the Illinois legislature. After his opponent delivered a long-winded speech, Lincoln stepped up and gave a speech that was less than seventy words long: "Gentlemen, Fellow-citizens: I presume you know who I am. I am humble Abraham Lincoln. I have been solicited by many friends to become a candidate for the legislature. My politics can be briefly stated. I am in favor of the internal improvement system, and a high protective tariff. These are my sentiments and political principles. If elected, I shall be thankful. If not, it will be all the same."[104]

Thirty-one years later, on November 19, 1863, President Lincoln went to the site of a Civil War battlefield in Gettysburg, Pennsylvania, to dedicate Soldiers' National Cemetery. Few people know that the featured speaker that day was not President Lincoln but famed Massachusetts orator Edward Everett. He spoke for two solid hours—an oration nearly 14,000 words long.

Then President Lincoln stood and spoke for two minutes—a speech consisting of only ten sentences totaling 268 words. It's a humble speech, in which the president says that the world "will little note, nor long remember what we say here." Like most of Lincoln's speeches, it does not contain the word "I." Instead, it speaks of the deeds of "these honored dead" and the collective duty of "us the living." Today, Edward Everett's two-hour speech is forgotten, but Lincoln's two-minute speech is memorized by schoolchildren.

Michael Maccoby mistakes Lincoln's confidence and ambition—a humble ambition to serve others and serve his country—for narcissistic hubris. In the process, Maccoby misses the profound humility of the Great Emancipator.

Gautam Mukunda, an assistant professor at Harvard Business School and author of *Indispensable: When Leaders Really Matter*, writes in *Fast Company*:

> *Of all the leaders I have studied, Lincoln is the one I am most certain was truly great. This is because Lincoln uniquely combined the highest levels of two seemingly antagonistic traits. Lincoln was both supremely confident and supremely humble.*
>
> *Confidence allows a leader to chart his or her own course, whatever others say. Humility lets a leader acknowledge the*

possibility that he or she is wrong, listen to
and take seriously those who disagree, and
by doing so avoid needless mistakes.[105]

The evidence of history aligns with Mukunda's assessment of Lincoln's confident humility, not Maccoby's claim of Lincoln's alleged "narcissism."

THE NARCISSISTIC PERSONALITY DISORDER

I don't believe there's such a thing as a "productive narcissist." The traits associated with narcissism—arrogance, excessive self-love, a sense of entitlement—are always destructive, not productive. In its most extreme forms, narcissism becomes a *personality disorder*—a diagnosable mental disorder that can cause an individual to behave in ways that are destructive to himself and to people around him, harming relationships and even harming society.

Many authorities believe that history's worst tyrants and criminals—Nero, Adolf Hitler, Josef Stalin, Mao Tse-Tung, Saddam Hussein, Moammar Qaddafi, cult leader Jim Jones, serial killer Ted Bundy, and mass murderer Charles Manson, to name a few—exhibited traits of the narcissistic personality disorder (NPD). The Mayo Clinic describes the traits of NPD:

- *Having an exaggerated sense of self-importance*
- *Expecting to be recognized as superior*

even without achievements that warrant it

- *Exaggerating your achievements and talents*
- *Being preoccupied with fantasies about success, power, brilliance, beauty or the perfect mate*
- *Believing that you are superior and can only be understood by or associate with equally special people*
- *Requiring constant admiration*
- *Having a sense of entitlement*
- *Expecting special favors and unquestioning compliance with your expectations*
- *Taking advantage of others to get what you want*
- *Having an inability or unwillingness to recognize the needs and feelings of others*
- *Being envious of others and believing others envy you*
- *Behaving in an arrogant or haughty manner*

Although some features of narcissistic personality disorder may seem like having confidence, it's not the same. Narcissistic personality disorder crosses the border of

healthy confidence into thinking so highly
of yourself that you put yourself on a
pedestal and value yourself more than you
value others.[106]

Many narcissistic business leaders or political leaders achieve great fame, wealth, and power—for a while. But the same self-aggrandizing drive that propels them to the top is often the Achilles' heel that leads to their downfall. Even Michael Maccoby recognizes this danger, warning: "Narcissistic leaders—even the most productive of them—can self-destruct and lead their organizations terribly astray."[107] Narcissistic leaders, Maccoby warns, don't listen to others, and they insulate themselves from criticism by surrounding themselves with yes-men. They are defensive and intolerant of dissent, they lack empathy, and they lack a conscience. They have a sense of entitlement and think that rules are for *other* people.

The more power you invest in a narcissistic leader, the greater the damage he can do. A narcissistic CEO might destroy a company. A narcissistic pastor might destroy a church. But what kind of damage might a narcissistic dictator or president do? What if you placed an army, a navy, or the nuclear launch codes in the hands of someone who listens to no one, punishes dissent, has no conscience, and obeys no moral law? We don't have to wonder. We've seen it before—when a narcissistic Nazi dictator plunged the world into a war that killed 80 million people.

Or take the example of Napoléon Bonaparte, emperor of France from 1804 to 1814. By 1811, Napoléon ruled the largest empire since the fall of Rome—and more than 70 million people owed their allegiance to him. A commoner who declared himself Emperor, Napoléon desperately wanted to marry a princess and authenticate his royal status, becoming the equal of the other crowned heads of Europe. In 1812, he asked Russian Czar Alexander I for the hand of his sister, Catherine Pavlovna, in marriage. Alexander refused. Napoléon then asked Alexander for the hand of another sister, Anna Pavlovna. Again, Alexander refused.

Infuriated, Napoléon assembled his Grande Armée of more than 450,000 men and, ignoring the advice of military advisers, launched an invasion of Russia. The war ended in disaster for France. Most of his soldiers died in battle or froze to death in the Russian winter, and only 40,000 French soldiers returned alive. Russian losses, both soldiers and civilians, were in the hundreds of thousands.

In 1814, Napoléon organized an army of 350,000 soldiers and sent them into battle against a coalition of nations—Russia, Prussia, Austria, Sweden, Great Britain, Spain, and Portugal. Napoléon's forces were defeated at the Battle of Leipzig, and Napoléon was forced to abdicate. He was exiled to Elba. In early 1815, Napoléon escaped from Elba with a force of 700 men.

He reached Paris on March 20 and declared himself emperor once more. He ruled for a period known as the Hundred Days. Then British and Prussian armies defeated Napoléon's forces at Waterloo on June 18, 1815, and Britain exiled Napoléon to the island of St. Helena in the mid-Atlantic, where he died in 1821.

Napoléon spent the lives of at least 860,000 French soldiers, plus countless enemy soldiers, in his wars of conquest. Leadership historians Henry Blackaby and Richard Blackaby observe that all those lives were sacrificed on the altar of Napoléon's narcissistic ego:

> *It could be argued that hundreds of thousands of Europeans died in one man's vain attempt to achieve satisfaction through the brutal acquisition of power and fame. Ego-driven people become desensitized to the suffering of others. It is acknowledged that few commanders suffered military casualties with greater indifference than Napoléon.*
>
> *The Duke of Wellington lamented the loss of thousands, but Napoléon boasted he would readily sacrifice a million soldiers to attain his goals.*[108]

The abuse of authority to serve a leader's narcissistic ego can destroy people and nations. That's the toxic legacy of narcissistic leadership.

The Humble Confidence of Churchill

Michael Maccoby calls Winston Churchill one of "history's greatest narcissistic leaders."[109] What evidence does he offer? None. Why does Maccoby make such an unsupported claim? I don't know. I have studied the life of Churchill, and I devoted a chapter of my book *21 Great Leaders* (Barbour, 2015) to Churchill. I think Maccoby makes the same mistake in assessing Churchill that he made with Lincoln. He mistakes the confidence of a great leader for the arrogance of a narcissist. But a closer look at Churchill's life will show, once again, that humble confidence is the foundation of leadership success.

Born into the family of the dukes of Marlborough, Winston Churchill was the son of Lord Randolph Churchill, a gifted political speaker, and Jennie Jerome Churchill, an American socialite. Winston was raised by a nanny and had little contact with his parents. In fact, his father rarely spoke to him and died at age forty-five. Young Winston believed that he, too, would die young and was driven to achieve success early in life.

In his youth, Churchill was afflicted with two speech impediments—a pronounced lisp and a severe stutter. His speech impediments make it all the more amazing that he was such an inspiring speaker in his later years. The Churchill Centre and Churchill Museum says it is a "myth" that Churchill stuttered,[110] but journalist Harold Begbie, who knew Churchill well, wrote in 1921:

> *Mr. Churchill is one of the most sensitive of prominent politicians, and it is only by the exercise of his remarkable courage that he has mastered this element of nervousness. Ambition has driven him onward, and courage has carried him through, but more often than the public thinks he has suffered sharply in his progress. The impediment of speech, which in his very nervous moments would almost make one think his mouth was roofless, would have prevented many men from even attempting to enter public life; it has always been a handicap to Mr. Churchill, but he has never allowed it to stop his way. . . .*
>
> *Mr. Churchill is more often fighting himself than his enemies.*[111]

Though Begbie didn't specifically call Churchill's impediment a stutter, that's exactly the impediment that emerges in "very nervous moments." And in the *Kansas City Star*, February 6, 1941, Louis J. Alber and Charles J. Rolo published a story headlined CHURCHILL HAS MASTERED A STUTTER AND A LISP TO BECOME AN ORATOR. They wrote:

Winston Churchill grew up with a lisp and a stutter, the result of a defect in his palate. It is characteristic of the man's perseverance that, despite this handicap, he has made himself one of the greatest orators of all time.

Churchill has never cured the lisp. And the stutter still breaks out when he gets excited—which is often.[112]

Churchill met his future wife, Clementine, at a party and proposed to her in August 1908; they wed the following month. Churchill held numerous political and cabinet positions during his decades-long career, including First Lord of the Admiralty. He planned the Gallipoli campaign of World War I, an ill-fated British-French effort to capture the Ottoman Empire's capital of Constantinople (now Istanbul). The failed campaign led to the death of nearly 57,000 soldiers of the United Kingdom and France, and a nearly equal loss of Ottoman lives. It was one of the few Ottoman victories of the war. The Gallipoli disaster forced Churchill out of the government, though he would later return in triumph.

During the 1930s, Churchill warned of the rising threat of Nazi Germany. His warnings were ignored as Hitler annexed Austria and parts of Czechoslovakia. In September 1939, Germany invaded Poland, igniting World War II. On January 20, 1940, Churchill gave a radio speech, "House of Many Mansions," promising liberation for the nations Hitler had subjugated: "The day will come when the joybells will ring again throughout Europe, and when victorious nations, masters not only of their foes but of themselves, will plan and build in justice, in tradition, and in freedom a house of many mansions where there will be room for all."[113] Four months later, on May 10, 1940, he became prime minister.

On May 13, the new prime minister stood before the House of Commons and delivered his "Blood, Toil, Tears, and Sweat" speech. The hall was electrified as he said, "You ask, what is our aim? I can answer in one word: It is *victory*, victory at all costs, victory in spite of all terror, victory, however long and hard the road may be."[114]

Churchill was an early proponent of what management expert Tom Peters calls "MBWA"—managing by wandering around. Immediately after becoming prime minister, Churchhill greeted crowds in the streets of London, where people could talk to him and even touch him. They shouted, "Good luck, Winnie! God bless you!" Churchill was moved by their expressions of support. He choked back tears as he entered the admiralty building, then he turned to an aide and said, "Poor people, poor people. They trust me, and I can give them nothing but disaster for quite a long time." [115] This was one of many demonstrations of Churchill's humble empathy for others.

Churchill's granddaughter, Celia Sandys, observes that both Churchill and his wartime nemesis, Adolf Hitler, were skilled public speakers with the ability to move the emotions of the masses. But there was a vast difference between Churchill and Hitler. Sandys said, "Hitler could persuade you that *he* could do anything, but. . .Churchill could persuade you that *you* could do anything." Her grandfather, she added, never employed speechwriters but always wrote his own speeches.[116]

It's true. A genuine narcissist like Hitler is concerned only about one thing: the almighty self. Hitler demanded the worship of the masses, and everything he said was calculated to enhance his godlike status in German society. Historian Patrick Romane observed:

> *Throughout his political life, Hitler's gifts for oratory. . .served to establish and embellish the cult of the Führer and the myth he consciously created of himself as an historic figure. Hitler cast his public speeches, his proclamations, his remarks at ceremonial occasions, and his participation in the great public spectacles of the Nazi calendar to perpetuate the aura of himself as a legendary figure, a "world historical genius," as he often referred to himself. Before the end of his life, Hitler completely subsumed his private identity into his public persona—the one, all-powerful*

*historic Führer, with whom Germany and
its fate were inextricably tied.*[117]

Political psychologist Jerrold M. Post warns that
the threat to society of narcissistic leadership didn't
die with Hitler. That threat is still with us today.
While humbly confident leaders (like Churchill)
seek to inspire people to overcome obstacles and
achieve greatness, narcissistic leaders deliver speeches
calculated only to elevate themselves. Post writes,
"Words do not convey deeply held beliefs for the
narcissist. Their only use is instrumental, to enhance
his personal position and gain admiration and support. *The only central and stable belief of the narcissist
is the centrality of the self. What is good for him is good
for his country.* . . . The individual comes to believe
that the national interest and national security are
in fact crucially contingent upon his reelection or
reappointment" (emphasis in the original).[118]

Like Lincoln, Churchill went out of his way to
gather advisers who challenged his thinking. Arrogant
narcissists prefer the company of yes-men and acolytes.
But Churchill—demonstrating authentic humility
the day after becoming prime minister—invited his
Labour Party opponent, Clement Attlee, to join a
coalition government. He also invited Conservative
Party leader Lord Halifax, who had strongly opposed
Churchill before the war, to remain as foreign secretary.

We see the humility of Churchill in the way he

put people at ease in his presence. A prime example: Sergeant James Allen Ward of the RAF's Seventy-Fifth New Zealand Squadron.

Sergeant Ward was the copilot of a Vickers Wellington twin-engine bomber on the night of July 7, 1941. As Ward and his crew returned from a bombing raid over Germany, they were attacked by a German fighter over Holland. Machine gun fire from the German plane wounded the tail-gunner, severed a fuel line, and set the aircraft's starboard wing on fire. In an amazing feat of heroism, Sergeant Ward tied a rope around his waist, crawled out onto the burning wing, and smothered the flames with canvas. Hours later, the bomber crash-landed in England and was destroyed, but every crewmember survived.

The following month, Prime Minister Winston Churchill awarded Sergeant Ward the Victoria Cross, England's highest decoration for heroism. As Sergeant Ward stood at attention in Churchill's office at No. 10 Downing Street, the prime minister tried to engage the young airman in conversation. Sergeant Ward's hands shook, and he could hardly speak.

"Young man," Churchill said, "you must feel very humble and awkward in my presence."

"Yes, sir," Sergeant Ward managed to stammer.

"Then you can imagine how humble and awkward I feel in yours."

With those humble words, Churchill put the young hero at ease.[119]

The war in Europe ended on May 8, 1945. As

crowds celebrated in the streets, Churchill came out on the balcony of the Ministry of Health and raised the "V for Victory" sign with two fingers. He spoke into a microphone, and his words echoed in the streets: "God bless you all! This is your victory!"

But the crowd shouted back, "No, it is yours!"

Churchill insisted on reflecting credit for the victory back to the people themselves. "It is the victory of the cause of freedom in every land," he said. "In all our long history we have never seen a greater day than this. Everyone, man or woman, has done their bit. Everyone has tried, none has flinched. Neither the long years, nor the dangers, nor the fierce attacks of the enemy, have in any way weakened the unbending resolve of the British nation. God bless you all."[120]

In 1954, in a televised celebration for his eightieth birthday, Churchill humbly reflected on the war years, saying, "I have never accepted what many people have kindly said—namely, that I inspired the nation. Their will was resolute and remorseless, and as it proved, unconquerable. It was the nation. . .that had the lion's heart. I had the luck to be called upon to give the roar."[121]

Those who would portray Churchill as narcissistic quote his witticisms as if he were serious. For example, Clement Attlee reported with amusement that Churchill once told him, "Of course I am an egotist. Where do you get if you aren't?" That line expresses confidence, not arrogance.

On another occasion, Churchill chided an assistant, Roy Howells, saying, "You were very rude to me, you know." Howells replied, "Yes, but you were rude, too." With a hint of a smile, Churchill shot back, "Yes, but I *am* a great man." Had Churchill truly been as arrogant as his critics portray him, Howells wouldn't have dared accuse him of rudeness.[122]

In September 1949, Norman McGowan applied to be Churchill's valet. Churchill shook McGowan's hand and said softly, "So you are Norman. You are going to look after me. . . . I think we will get along all right." McGowan later recalled, "It was the shortest interview I had ever had."[123]

McGowan wrote a book, *My Years with Churchill*, a personal portrait of the leader he came to know fondly as "the Great Man" and "my Guv'nor." As you read McGowan's first-person account, you can't help being impressed with the essential humility of Churchill. "I have never heard him boast," McGowan wrote, "but often detected in him an understatement."[124] McGowan also observed the kindness of the Great Man: "Sir Winston Churchill has no malice in his character. He is totally incapable of rancor."[125] Of Churchill's compassion, McGowan wrote:

> *My little daughter had been born incapacitated. I had made no mention of this, for it was to my mind a personal burden of no concern to my employers.*

But with the child living on the estate Mr. Churchill soon saw the matter for himself. He wanted to ask Lord Moran for advice and he inferred in no uncertain terms that money was no object in obtaining the best possible medical aid.

It so happened. . .that one of the best specialists in the country was a consultant at the hospital in Westerham, so that we could have the attention for our child that she needed through the National Health Service and at a hospital conveniently near.

My Guv'nor satisfied himself that this was true and so the generous help that I could have asked for without question was not needed.[126]

McGowan noted that Churchill found "unctuous flattery" annoying, though he always displayed "the courtesy with a stranger to disguise the fact." On one occasion a woman approached Churchill and gushed, "Doesn't it thrill you, Mr. Churchill, to know that every time you make a speech the hall is packed to overflowing?"

"It is quite flattering," Churchill replied humbly, "but whenever I feel this way I always remember that if instead of making a political speech I was being hanged, the crowd would be twice as big."[127]

Churchill enjoyed it when others (such as his son Randolph) would verbally spar with him. McGowan recalled, "Those who made cheap jibes simply for notoriety, or possibly on the grounds of personal jealousy, created nothing but contempt in his mind, but others who argued the points with him from their hearts he treated with respect and regarded with something close to affection as adversaries worthy of his attention." [128]

McGowan observed that Churchill never finished smoking his cigars. He always left them half smoked in an ashtray. Churchill gave McGowan special orders to collect the unsmoked cigars in a box, which were given to Mr. Kearns, the gardener. Kearns put the unburnt tobacco in his pipe. Whenever Churchill saw the gardener around the estate, he would always ask if he was getting his regular supply of tobacco.

Churchill demonstrated a touching concern for everyone who worked for him. On one occasion, McGowan accompanied Churchill to the United States. While in New York City, Churchill dined with his friend the duke of Windsor, and McGowan decided to go see the city lights. As he was about to leave, the secretary stopped him and said, "Mr. Churchill wants to see you."

Leaving the duke of Windsor at the dining table, Churchill took McGowan aside. "Norman," he said, "I wanted to tell you to be careful in this New York traffic. It's very dangerous. I was knocked down here some years ago."

These thoughtful words, McGowan reflected, were "typical of my Guv'nor's consideration."[129]

On January 15, 1965, Churchill suffered a severe stroke. On the morning of Sunday, January 24, he passed into history, leaving behind a legacy of humble confidence that is an example to you and me.

STEPS TO GREATER CONFIDENCE—AND DEEPER HUMILITY

"Great leaders don't need to act tough," said Simon Sinek, author of *Leaders Eat Last*. "Their confidence and humility serve to underscore their toughness." Finding that perfect balance of confidence and humility isn't easy. We all have a tendency to skew a little too far one way or the other. A little too much confidence— and we find ourselves in arrogance territory. Too much humility and we veer into unhealthy self-deprecation. Here are some practical ways to maintain a fine-tuned balance of humility and confidence:

1. *Reflect on your confidence level and ask yourself, "Am I overconfident—or under-confident?"* Do you fail to assert yourself when it's time to negotiate a raise, the price of a car, or the terms of a contract? Do you have a long list of projects or goals you've always wanted to accomplish—but haven't? Do you hesitate in times of crisis or decision-making? Then you are probably under-confident—and there are steps you can take to

build your confidence.

In conversations, do you tend to talk about yourself and your accomplishments while expressing no interest or curiosity about others? When people tell you a story from their own experience, do you "top" their story with one of your own? Do you treat restaurant servers, drivers, desk clerks, and other service people as if their feelings don't matter? Do you give more courteous treatment to people who can do things for you? If so, your confidence may have turned to arrogance and selfishness. There are steps you can take to increase your humility.

2. *Take steps to increase your healthy confidence.* First step: Walk and talk with confidence. Pay attention to your body language. Stand up straight, pull your shoulders back, look people in the eye, and smile confidently. When you stand and speak confidently, you'll actually feel your confidence level rising—and people will respond to your confident body language.

Second step: Silence negative voices. Don't beat yourself down verbally or mentally. Instead of berating yourself when you make a mistake, learn to laugh at your foibles—then tell yourself, "I can do this." If people in your life verbally demean you, consider confronting their behavior—or limiting their involvement in your life. Don't let toxic people diminish your confidence.

Third step: Take risks. Don't be reckless, don't take

foolish gambles—but make a deliberate habit of doing the things that scare you. You may fail sometimes, but that's okay. When you succeed, you'll ratchet up your confidence. As your confidence increases, you'll feel more comfortable taking bigger risks. In general, the greater the risk, the bigger the payoff. So learn a new skill, take on a new project, accept a new challenge, and see it through to completion.

Fourth step: Look to the future. Let go of the past, especially past failures. Don't beat yourself up and say, "I failed." Instead, build yourself up and say, "I learned something. This lesson will boost me to success."

Fifth step: Learn to accept compliments gracefully. People with low confidence often feel unworthy of compliments. People with healthy confidence accept praise but don't dwell on it.

3. *Take steps to increase your humility.* First step: Focus on others. This doesn't mean your needs and priorities are unimportant. It simply means you recognize the needs and priorities of others. It means you make a continual effort to notice people, listen to them, empathize with them, and treat them with courtesy and respect.

Second step: Don't take yourself too seriously. Learn to laugh at yourself. Set aside your pride. Learn to accept constructive criticism instead of defending yourself.

Third step: Accept your limitations. You don't have

to pretend to be all-knowing, all-wise, or all-competent. If someone asks you a question and you don't know the answer, say, "I don't know, I'll find out." Writing in *Harvard Business Review*, Jeanine Prime and Elizabeth Salib observed, "When leaders humbly admit that they don't have all the answers, they create space for others to step forward and offer solutions."[130]

Fourth step: Focus on serving, not on self. One of the best ways to forget your troubles is to serve others. Become the solution to other people's problems, the answer to other people's prayers. In the process of helping and serving others, you'll find a new perspective on your own problems. You become less self-centered, more others-centered.

The key to humble confidence is to see yourself realistically. You're not greater than other people, but you're not less than others, either. Maintain a balanced view of yourself. As someone once said, "Don't let failure go to your heart—and don't let success go to your head." That's the balance we need—a perfect balance of confidence and humility.

Confidence, Not Arrogance

One day in July 2000, I sat down at my desk and checked my voicemail. "Mr. Williams," said a soft-spoken voice, "this is John Wooden, the former basketball coach at UCLA." I was amazed—first, because the greatest coach in the history of sports had left a message on my voicemail, and second, because he actually thought he needed to remind me who he was. He was calling to give his recommendation for a UCLA trainer who was applying for a job with the Magic. He closed the message with these words: "I have enjoyed reading your books very much. Good-bye."

Sometime later, I called Coach Wooden and got his answering machine. I left a message, asking for his blessing on a book I wanted to write called *How to Be Like Coach Wooden*. He called me back and again left a message on my voicemail. As he had the previous time, he began, "Mr. Williams, this is John Wooden, the former basketball coach at UCLA." Then he added, "I'm not worthy of a project like you describe—but if you would like to write it, you have my permission." That's the voice of humility.

In writing that book, I became personally acquainted with Coach Wooden and had a number of opportunities to visit with him at his Encino, California, condominium. Every time I was in his presence, I marveled at the way he modeled that perfect balance of confidence and humility. He wouldn't hesitate to give you the benefit of his accumulated wisdom, yet he was always gentle and self-effacing, never condescending.

When a rare human being like Coach Wooden comes along, the world takes notice. Coach always seemed unaware of his greatness. He seemed shy and even embarrassed when people gushed over his accomplishments. On one occasion, he was the featured speaker at an event and the emcee introduced him with overflowing praise. Coach Wooden rose and humbly said, "I hope the good Lord will forgive my introducer for over-praising me, and me for enjoying it so much."[131]

Coach Wooden once offered excellent advice for maintaining that delicate balance of confidence and humility. He said, "Confidence must be monitored so that it does not spoil or rot and turn into arrogance . . . . I have never gone into a game assuming victory. All opponents have been respected, none feared. I taught those under my supervision to do the same. This reflects confidence, not arrogance. Arrogance will bring you down by your own hands."[132]

Confidence plus humility is the secret formula for greatness. It's so simple, yet even leadership experts fail to understand. They mistake confidence for narcissism. I know you won't make the same mistake. You know the secret. You can find that balance. By tempering your confidence with humility, you will go far—and you will leave a legacy of humble confidence to future generations.

6

Humility as a Communication Style

Do you wish people to think well of you?
Don't speak well of yourself.

—Mathematician-philosopher Blaise Pascal

On January 15, 2016—Martin Luther King Jr.'s birthday—I was at Northwest Arkansas Airport, near Fayetteville, preparing to board a plane for Atlanta. I was on my way home to Orlando after a speaking engagement in Arkansas. As I was boarding, I happened to look behind me, and who did I see but Congressman John Lewis, the representative for Georgia's Fifth Congressional District. Congressman Lewis is the last living member of the "Big Six" of the civil rights movement of the 1960s (the other five were Roy Wilkins, A. Philip Randolph, Whitney Young, James Farmer, and Dr. Martin Luther King Jr.). Lewis had headed the Student Nonviolent Coordinating Committee and was one of the chief organizers of the March on Washington on August 28, 1963, when Dr. King delivered his "I Have a Dream" speech.

I greeted him and introduced myself. I told him we had met once before, years earlier, and he seemed to remember me. He was cordial and gracious, and we had a few moments to exchange pleasantries before it was time to board.

During the flight to Atlanta, I marveled at the amazing timing of this chance meeting: here I was on Martin Luther King Jr.'s birthday, and I was on the same plane with a man who had marched with Dr. King. I got off the plane and waited in the concourse for Congressman Lewis to deplane. When I saw him coming down the corridor, I called him aside and said, "Could I speak with you for a few moments? I'm eager to hear some of your insights on Dr. King's leadership strengths."

An aide tried to hurry Congressman Lewis along, but he said, "I have a few moments for Mr. Williams."

I told the congressman that my mother and sister and I had been in the crowd on the National Mall for the March on Washington. "Dr. King's words were like thunder," I said. "He impacted my life and changed the course of history. Congressman, what was it about Dr. King that made him such a great leader?"

"Martin Luther King," he said, "had the ability to inspire people so that they would believe and follow. He was a teacher and a motivator who spoke with authority, and his authority was rooted in humility. I remember being fifteen years old and listening to Dr. King on the radio. He inspired me and motivated me to get involved and make a difference. I wouldn't be the person I am today without Dr. King as my teacher and role model."

I had my notebook out and I jotted down his thoughts as he shared them with me. He mentioned that he was the youngest one on the platform during that hot summer day in 1963. Then he added, "The next time you are in Washington, come by my office. I have a photo of everyone who was on that platform that day, and they all signed the picture. I'm the only one still living. Come by anytime. I'll show you the picture." He gave me his card, and we parted.

I could not have had a more memorable experience on Dr. King's birthday than to meet and speak with Congressman Lewis and to soak up his insights on Dr. King's influence and greatness. And the key insight I picked up from Congressman Lewis was that Dr. King communicated with authority, and his authority was rooted in his humility.

Later, as I reflected on my encounter with Congressman Lewis, I recalled an anecdote from my chapter on Dr. King in *21 Great Leaders*. Young Martin was a gifted student who had skipped the ninth and twelfth grades and was accepted into college without a high school diploma. He possessed a great intellect and a powerful vocabulary. In his early preaching career, he tended to show off his vast knowledge by using big words and literary quotations.

Martin's father, known as "Daddy King," was also a preacher. When Martin began to show off his erudition during a sermon, Daddy King would warn him against "gaining altitude" and becoming grandiose. The elder King would sit in the front pew as Martin preached and would occasionally whisper, "Keep it simple, son, keep it simple." In this way, Daddy King helped young Martin learn humility as a communicator—and Martin's humility lent power and authority to his message. Listen to recordings of his speeches, and you can sense the fine-tuned balance of authority and humility as he speaks.

The way we communicate, whether in individual conversations or in front of audiences, has a huge impact on our success. Humility is more than an attitude. Humility is a communication style.

And humility speaks with authority.

POWERFUL, PROFANE, AND HUMBLE

I can imagine someone reading this book and saying, "What about General Patton? Doesn't he disprove your claim that humility is the secret ingredient of success? He was one of the most successful military leaders in history—and one of the most egotistical."

It's true that General George S. Patton Jr. was amazingly successful. Under his command, the Seventh Army invaded and liberated Sicily in July 1943. In 1944, after the D-Day invasion, Patton took command of the Third Army. His troops routed the Germans in the Battle of the Bulge, and by the time the Nazis surrendered on May 8, 1945, Patton had captured or liberated 81,522 square miles of territory in France, Belgium, Luxembourg, Austria, Czechoslovakia, and Germany. His forces liberated more than 12,000 European cities, and he never lost a battle. In fact,

General Patton led his forces farther, took more enemy prisoners, and captured more territory in a shorter period of time than any other leader in military history. He was arguably the most successful general who ever lived.

But was he truly arrogant and egotistical, as some claim? Or has he been misunderstood? One Patton biographer, Earle Rice Jr., described General Patton as a human paradox:

> *He was and remains many things to many people—at alternate times crude and cultured; cruel and compassionate; egotistical and self-effacing; confident on the outside, uncertain of his ability on the inside; a flamboyant, pistol-packing, cursing leader of men as well as a sensitive, scholarly, poetic student of history and the arts. His complex personality seemed always to exhibit two sides in all things, each in total opposition to the other. Yet somehow his mix of opposing characteristics produced an uncommon genius on the battlefield.*[133]

And another Patton biographer, Porter B. Williamson, author of *General Patton's Principles for Life and Leadership*, served with General Patton at the Desert Training Center in the Mojave Desert.

Williamson became well acquainted with General Patton while serving with him. He reported that the life lessons he learned from Patton have guided him in his life, his career, and his battle with cancer. Williamson disputes the portrayal of Patton as arrogant:

> *Several Patton authors have called the General arrogant, flamboyant, and foolhardy. These authors failed to understand that the pistols, the arrogant lectures, and the flamboyant actions were the carefully rehearsed and planned actions of a man who knew how to lead men into combat—to face the enemy and death. No writer who called General Patton foolhardy understood the importance of immediate pursuit of a retreating enemy.*
>
> *No author can adequately portray the complexity of the man; an iron will combined with humility, a surprising sense of humor with a boyish grin, and a deep religious faith.*[134]

One of Patton's most important skills was his ability to motivate and energize his troops through his speeches. Shortly before D-Day, General Patton toured army bases west of London. At each stop, the man known as "Old Blood and Guts" strode to the microphone dressed in a starched uniform, with highly polished boots, a mirror-finished helmet, and a Colt .45 holstered at his hip. Then he delivered what has come to be known simply as the Speech.

I've read the text of that speech, and it is powerful and profane—and it is also humble. More than fifty times, he uses the word *you*. Throughout that speech, he encourages and praises his men. The word *I* only appears ten times in the speech—and never in an egotistical way. When he says "I," he does so to praise and motivate his men, as in, "I actually pity those poor so-and-sos we're going up against."

Patton talked about winning. "Americans love a winner," he said. And, "The very thought of losing is hateful to an American." He talked about teamwork. "An army is a team. It lives, sleeps, eats, and fights as a team." And he talked about the vital contribution of every individual soldier. "Every single man in this army plays a vital role. Don't ever let up. Don't ever think that your job is unimportant. Every man has a job to do and he must do it. Every man is a vital link in the great chain. . . . Every man does his job. Every man serves the whole. Every department, every unit, is important in the vast scheme of this war."

Like all great communicators, Patton was a storyteller, and he enlivened the Speech with inspiring anecdotes. He told about an American soldier bravely doing a dangerous, thankless job. "One of the bravest men I ever saw," he said, "was a fellow on top of a telegraph pole in the midst of a furious fire fight in Tunisia." Patton shouted to the man, "What are you doing up there at a time like this? Isn't that a little unhealthy right about now?" The man replied that the wire needed to be fixed. "Don't those planes strafing the road bother you?" asked Patton. "No, sir," the man replied, "but you sure do!"

"Now, there was a real man," Patton concluded with humble admiration, "a real soldier. There was a man who devoted all he had to his duty, no matter how seemingly insignificant his duty might appear at the time, no matter how great the odds."[135]

Great leaders like Dr. King and General Patton communicate with authority, not arrogance. Their authority is rooted in confidence and conviction, tempered with humility.

Patton trained leaders, and his advice to the leaders he trained was, first, *speak with confidence*. He once said, "I can tell a commander by the way he speaks. He does not have to swear as much as I do, but he has to speak so that no one will refuse to follow his order. Certain words will make you sound like a staff officer and not a commander. A good commander will never express an opinion! A commander knows! No one cares what your opinion is! Never use the words, 'In my opinion, I believe, I think, or I guess,' and never say 'I don't think!' Every man who hears you speak must know what you want. You can be wrong, but never be in doubt when you speak! Any doubt or fear in your voice and the troops can feel it. Another thing: Never give a command in a sitting position unless you are on a horse or on top of a tank!"[136]

But Patton didn't merely teach communicating with confidence. He also taught that leaders should *communicate with humility*—and that means *leaders should listen*. He put it this way: "Always talk with the troops! They know more about the war than anybody. Make them tell you all of their gripes. Make sure they know we are doing everything we can to help them. The soldiers will have to win the war. We cannot do it. Talk with them. They will not trust you if you do not trust them."[137]

Great leaders communicate confidently yet humbly—and one of the most important signs of humility is the ability to listen.

ADDING HUMILITY TO THE LIST

One of the greatest of all American success stories is Benjamin Franklin—author, newspaper publisher, scientist, inventor, and statesman. He is the only founding father who signed all four documents that established the United States—the Declaration of Independence, the Treaty of Alliance with France, the Treaty of Paris, and the US Constitution. Though he owned two slaves for a time, he freed them both and became president of the Pennsylvania Abolition Society. Franklin attributed all of his accomplishments to a lifetime commitment to a set of moral virtues, with humility chief among them.

When Franklin was in his twenties, he set a goal of attaining moral excellence so that he could become successful in life. He began by drawing up a list of virtues—moral traits that he wanted to build into his life. In his *Autobiography*, he recalled:

> *My list of virtues contain'd at first but twelve; but a Quaker friend having kindly informed me that I was generally thought proud; that my pride show'd itself frequently in conversation; that I was not content with being in the right when discussing any point, but was overbearing, and rather insolent, of which he convinc'd me by mentioning several instances; I determined endeavouring to cure myself, if I could. . .and I added Humility to my list.*[138]

In conversations, Franklin made it a rule to stop contradicting other people and proving them wrong. He avoided dogmatic language (such as "certainly" and "undoubtedly") and began using more humble expressions ("I imagine" or "it appears"). As a result of adopting a more modest communication style, Franklin discovered he became more influential and persuasive. "The modest way in which I propos'd my opinions," he said, "procur'd them a readier reception and less contradiction."[139]

Over the years, Franklin continued to practice these virtues until they became indelible habits. He became known as a wise elder statesman who could bring consensus out of conflict. Historian Ralph Louis Ketcham describes Franklin's humble influence when, at age eighty-one, he served as a delegate to the Constitutional Convention of 1787:

> *His universal fame and legendary sagacity made failure seem much less likely; he seemed to give his colleagues courage to have great expectations. Furthermore, his was a respected voice able over and over again to soothe heated tempers and suggest constructive compromises. . . . During the bitter fight over representation, he cooled tempers by making his famous proposal that the sessions be opened with prayer, and a few days later, upon his motion, the Convention adopted the "Great Compromise" that the states be represented equally in the Senate and the people equally in the House.*
>
> *On the final working day of the Convention, in a speech which has become a revered part of the American political tradition, he urged each member to "doubt a little of his own Infallibility"*

*and despite reservations sign the
Constitution. . . . In teaching the habit of
accommodation and the value of accord
Franklin placed indispensable principles
at the foundation of the union of free
states.*[140]

It's sobering to realize that, if Benjamin Franklin had not learned the art of communicating with humility in his early life, he might not have become the humble voice of conciliation at the Constitutional Convention of 1787—and our form of government might look very different today as a result. Franklin's humility—his willingness to doubt his own infallibility—left an indelible mark on the US Constitution. His humble style of communication helped shape the world we live in today.

Another American leader who understood the power of humility in leadership communication was Ronald Reagan. One of his central goals as president was to dismantle the Berlin Wall. From the day he first heard that the Soviet Union and East Germany were building the Wall in August 1961, he hated it. He began speaking out against the Wall soon after it was built. He called for its destruction during a televised debate with Robert F. Kennedy in 1967 and in a May 1968 speech in Miami.

Once, during a tour of Europe with several advisers, he visited the Berlin Wall and glared with visible anger at the guard towers and gray concrete barriers that held the people of East Berlin imprisoned in their own city. Reagan told his traveling companions, "We have got to find a way to knock this thing down."[141]

After his inauguration in 1981, President Reagan pursued a two-pronged strategy. In his public speeches, he made strong, confident demands, such as his famous declaration at the Brandenburg Gate, June 12, 1987: "Mr. Gorbachev, tear down this wall!" In private conversations with Mr. Gorbachev, President Reagan appealed to the Soviet leader in more humble terms. A key example was the Reagan-Gorbachev summit of May 29, 1988, in Moscow. The two leaders sat together in St. Catherine Hall in the Kremlin. Mr. Reagan described their conversation in his 1990 autobiography, *An American Life*:

> *I said Americans were very encouraged by the changes occurring in the Soviet Union. . . . And, for all the changes that Gorbachev had made, I said, wouldn't it be a good idea to tear down the Berlin Wall? Nothing in the West symbolized the differences between it and the Soviet Union more than the Wall, I said; its removal would be seen as a gesture symbolizing that the Soviet Union wanted to join the broader community of nations.*

*Well, Gorbachev listened and
seemed to take in my opinions; from his
expression I knew he didn't like some of
the things I was saying, but he didn't try
to say anything harsh in rebuttal. . . . In
time, the Wall came tumbling down.*[142]

Gorbachev repeatedly resisted Ronald Reagan's strong public demands and his humble private appeals. Eventually, events spun out of Gorbachev's control, and the people took matters into their own hands and opened the Wall in November 1989. For reasons that are still a mystery, the East German government chose not to crack down on the dissidents and protesters who opened the Wall. Official demolition of the Berlin Wall began the following year.

In 1990, the Norwegian Nobel Committee awarded the Peace Prize to Mikhail Gorbachev. That's right, they gave the Peace Prize to the man who had fought hard to keep the Berlin Wall standing. The Committee passed over Ronald Reagan, the man who had actually fought to dismantle that Wall. President Reagan received no credit for the accomplishment— and never complained about not receiving credit. As his elder son, Michael Reagan, explained in *Lessons My Father Taught Me*:

*My father wasn't hungry for praise and
applause. He just wanted to achieve the*

*goal. One reason my father was willing to
let Mikhail Gorbachev take all the credit
was that he knew that Gorbachev needed
to look like a hero and a leader to his own
people, or he would be undermined in his
own country. So Dad was willing to give
Gorbachev the credit if it would enable
Gorbachev to relax the restrictions on the
people of East Germany.*

*Throughout his eight years as
president, my father kept a brass plaque
on the Resolute desk in the Oval Office
that read: "There is no limit to what
a man can do or where he can go if he
doesn't mind who gets the credit." That
was not a mere platitude. That was
literally how he lived his life.*[143]

The essential humility of Mr. Reagan is exemplified
by his California ranch, which he called Rancho del
Cielo ("Heaven's Ranch"). As president, he received
many official guests (including Gorbachev, Queen
Elizabeth II, and Margaret Thatcher) at the 688-acre
ranch in the Santa Ynez Mountains. Visitors were
often amazed at the humble fifteen hundred–square-
foot Spanish-style ranch house that Reagan remodeled
with his own hands after leaving office as governor of
California. Michael Reagan explained, "My father was
a humble man who didn't feel any need to impress

other leaders with ostentatious surroundings."[144]

When President Reagan received praise or credit, he tended to share that with the people who helped him—including the American people who elected him. His farewell address to the nation, delivered from the Oval Office on January 11, 1989, was a masterpiece of humility. Reflecting on his nickname, "The Great Communicator," he said:

> *I never thought it was my style or the words I used that made a difference: it was the content. I wasn't a great communicator, but I communicated great things, and they didn't spring full bloom from my brow, they came from the heart of a great nation—from our experience, our wisdom, and our belief in the principles that have guided us for two centuries. . . .*
>
> *My friends: We did it. We weren't just marking time. We made a difference. We made the city stronger, we made the city freer, and we left her in good hands. All in all, not bad, not bad at all.*[145]

If you listen to political speeches today, you usually hear the personal pronoun "I" a lot, as in "I accomplished this" or "I initiated that." Reagan's "I" statements are usually statements of humility: "I wasn't a great communicator. . . ." Whenever he talked about great accomplishments, he always used the plural pronoun "we," as in, "We made a difference." That's humility talking. And as Michael Reagan said of his father and of every communicator of humble confidence, "The first trait of a good human being is humility."[146]

THE HUMBLY ASSERTIVE WOMAN

Financial journalist Maria Bartiromo has enjoyed a successful career at CNN, CNBC, and Fox News. In *The 10 Laws of Enduring Success*, she writes about business communication, observing that humility and assertiveness go hand in hand:

> *Some of the greatest people I know are also the most humble. Humility doesn't mean being wishy-washy, or letting others run over you in their climb to the top. It's merely the understanding that you're human. People with humility are extremely appealing. . . . We enjoy it when people can laugh at themselves. We dislike finger-pointers and sentence parsers— those who are always looking out for their image. Without humility, you can never see the truth about yourself and others.*
>
> *I grew up with the poem "If," by Rudyard Kipling. It always inspired me. "If" is in part a poem about humility—*

about understanding your place in the world. My favorite line is: "If you can trust yourself when all men doubt you, / But make allowance for their doubting, too." In other words, believe in yourself, but don't think you're the center of the universe.[147]

It's unfair, but true: in order to succeed, women often have to work harder than men to maintain a crucial balance between confidence and humility. Display too much confidence in your speech and actions, and some people will label you "overly aggressive." But display too much humility, and your contributions may go unnoticed.

Maggie Wilderotter, CEO of Frontier Communications, says that humble assertiveness is a key strategy women can use to overcome the "old boy network" and advance in their careers. Many women, she says, "think the myth is true, that if they just do a good job and work hard, they'll get recognized. That's not the case."

Wilderotter recalls making some strong points during a meeting, yet no one in the meeting would acknowledge her ideas. Then, a few minutes later, one of the male executives spoke up and made exactly the same points she had made. "When that happened," she recalled, "I stopped the conversation and said, 'Do you realize I said that ten minutes ago?' Women have to take responsibility for the dynamic around them;

you can't just say 'Woe is me.' "[148]

To be assertive is to communicate your own needs to others. To be humble is to be sensitive to the needs of others. Successful people are humble and assertive at the same time—helping to meet the needs of others while asserting their own needs in the process. When we operate by principles of humble assertiveness, everyone wins.

One successful woman who found the perfect balance of assertiveness and humility was Mother Teresa. She achieved so much because she communicated effectively, boldly, yet humbly. Church leaders, business leaders, and political leaders respected and even feared this little nun from Albania because she knew what she wanted—and she communicated what she wanted persuasively and effectively.

A few days before Christmas 1985, Mother Teresa visited the infamous Sing Sing Correctional Facility in Ossining, New York. There she met three prisoners infected with AIDS. These three men, age twenty-seven to thirty-six, were serving sentences for robbery. They reminded Mother Teresa of the beggars with leprosy she cared for in Calcutta, India.

She decided to build a hospice for terminally ill AIDS patients, and she would locate it at St. Veronica's Catholic Church in the West Village. But she needed help. So she went to the office of then-Mayor Ed Koch and asked him for financial aid and regulatory assistance. She planned to start with the three prisoners she had met at Sing Sing.

Mayor Koch called Governor Mario Cuomo and told him that Mother Teresa needed help getting her hospice started. Mother Teresa added that she had plans for an expanded hospice facility in the future, then she asked, "Governor Cuomo, would you like to pay for it?"

Before he realized what he was saying, Cuomo said, "Okay."

Mother Teresa turned to Mayor Koch and said, "Today is Monday. I plan to open the hospice on Wednesday. Can you arrange to waive the permit requirements?"

Mayor Koch replied, "As long as you don't make me wash the floors."[149]

Mother Teresa weighed ninety-eight pounds, consisting of equal parts confidence and humility. The combination was irresistible. The mayor of New York and the governor of New York felt they had been flattened by a steamroller in a nun's habit. They simply couldn't say no to her.

Born in 1910, Mother Teresa grew up fascinated with missionary work. By age twelve, she vowed to dedicate her life to serving God and the poor. At age eighteen, she joined the Sisters of Loreto. The following year, she began her novitiate training in Darjeeling, India, taking vows as a nun in 1931. She took the name "Sister Teresa" after Saint Thérèse de Lisieux (1873–1897), the patron saint of missionaries. For nearly two decades, she taught at Saint Mary's convent school in Calcutta, becoming headmistress in 1944.

On September 10, 1946, Sister Teresa was traveling by train to a spiritual retreat in the mountains of India. Along the way, she experienced a series of inner conversations and heard the voice of Jesus speaking to her, revealing His heart of love for the poor and sick. "Come," Jesus said to her, "be my light." For the rest of her life, she called that day her "Inspiration Day." Biographer Joseph Langford observed, "Though no one knew it at the time, Sister Teresa had just become *Mother* Teresa."[150]

In 1948, one year after India won its independence from British rule, Mother Teresa became a naturalized citizen of India and began her work among the poor. She devised creative approaches to funding her work—approaches that combined confidence and humility into a disarming and persuasive communicating style.

On one occasion, Mother Teresa went to a Calcutta grocery store that catered to the rich. She had no money—but she wasn't going to let a little thing like that stop her. She proceeded to fill two shopping carts with food, about $800 worth of groceries. Then she took the shopping carts to the cashier.

After the cashier had totaled up the grocery bill, Mother Teresa announced loudly, "I have no money to pay for these groceries. But I am buying food for poor, starving people—and I am not moving out of this line until the other patrons in this store come up with the donations to pay for this food."

There were quite a few people in line behind her, and they were eager to check out. They grumbled—but they took up a collection and Mother Teresa left with her groceries, fully paid for.[151]

Mother Teresa's ability to communicate with absolute confidence plus absolute humility enabled her to do great things for the poor of Calcutta. She learned that the city government wanted a solution to the problem of destitute and dying people in the city streets. So she went to the city officials and offered them a deal. "Give me a house, expense-free and tax-free, and I will take your destitute and dying people off the streets."[152]

She used this same confident-humble approach to charm donors, to recruit volunteers, and to get her way with government officials. In this way, she and her organization, The Missionaries of Charity, established clinics for people with Hansen's disease (leprosy), orphanages for abandoned children, and hospices for the dying—first in India, but eventually around the world.

Mother Teresa easily could have been a powerful CEO or politician. Her soft-as-mist humility combined with titanium-steel confidence made her an unstoppable communicator. Father Dwight Longenecker, an Anglican priest, recalls just how forceful this humble little nun could be.

Both Father Dwight and his friend Father James

grew up in India. Both lived in England, and in 1985, they took up a collection for Mother Teresa's mission. They set off on a journey to India. Arriving in Calcutta, they went to the mission house and presented the check to a nun at the front desk. The nun took the check to Mother Teresa.

Moments later, Father Dwight and Father James were surprised and delighted to see Mother Teresa emerge, greeting them warmly. She said, "Have you come to give your life in service to God's holy poor?"

The priests had not expected to be recruited by Mother Teresa. "We're Anglican priests from England," Father Dwight replied.

"We have many people working with us from England," she said. "Perhaps you will stay and work for just a few years?"

"We have parishes in England we need to return to."

"I understand," she said. "Go in peace, and thank you for coming."

Mother Teresa's simple, humble question was so compelling that, for years afterward, Father Dwight looked back on that day and asked himself, "What if. . . ?"[153]

In 1996, Mother Teresa suffered a number of health setbacks—a fall that broke her collarbone, heart surgery, and congestive heart failure. In March 1997, she stepped down as head of the society she had founded. She died on September 5, 1997. She left behind a legacy of caring and an example of how to achieve great goals by communicating with humble confidence.

How to Communicate with Confident Humility

People of confident humility have nothing to prove, nothing to hide, and no need to brag, exaggerate, or impress anyone. They are free to be exactly who they are, no more, no less. Rick Warren once said, "Humility is not denying your strengths. Humility is being honest about your weaknesses."[154] Here are some practical ways you can increase your influence and success by communicating confidently and humbly:

1. *Avoid the appearance of bragging.* Confident people don't need to brag, and humble people don't want to. Let your work do the talking.

Braggarts are unpleasant to be around. Some braggarts find ways to disguise their bragging. Some disguise it as a complaint: "I'm so sore! But that's what I get for running five miles this morning." Some disguise it as an apology: "Oops, sorry my tee shot landed on the green while you guys were putting!" And then there's the "humble brag," the brag disguised as humility, as when the job interviewee says, "My greatest weakness? I guess I'd have to say it's that I work too hard, I'm too much of a perfectionist, and I'm far too easy to get along with for my own good."

People can see through disguised bragging—and it's not attractive. If you're going to brag, you're better off bragging boldly than trying to disguise it. There are times when it's okay to toot your own horn—in a polite, humble manner.

But avoid disguised bragging and "humble bragging." Braggarts give off the scent of desperation and insecurity. The more humbly confident you are, the more comfortable you will be as you let your work speak for itself.

2. *Invite criticism, and don't defend yourself.* Genuinely humble people are open to constructive criticism, suggestions, and correction. Only the arrogant think they know it all. If someone cares about you enough to risk telling you a painful truth, drop your defenses. It's human nature to deflect criticism, but humility requires that we be willing to hear the worst about ourselves so we can achieve the best. That's how we grow and succeed.

3. *Celebrate the achievements of others.* Arrogant people celebrate their own successes; humble people celebrate when others triumph. Feelings of jealousy or envy indicate you need to work on your humility. Humble people don't compare themselves to others, and they aren't jealous of the success that others have earned. There are plenty of opportunities for success to go around. When others succeed, be happy for them—and mean it. Stay humble. Your time will come.

4. *Practice your listening skills.* Humble people are great listeners. Listening to others conveys caring and enables you to bridge differences with others. Give people your full attention. Look them in the eye and give them verbal feedback—"Really? . . . Right! . . . Exactly." Build a habit of "reflective listening," repeating back a person's key points in your own words. This way you show the other person you hear them and you value their thoughts and opinions: "As I understand it, you're saying. . ."

Master interviewer Larry King once explained why listening is such an important aspect of communicating: "I remind myself every morning: Nothing I say this day will teach me anything. So if I'm going to learn, I must do it by listening."[155]

What if people say something you disagree with? Hear them out. Avoid tuning out while you formulate your arguments. Listen, patiently and humbly. Before responding, make sure you have heard and understood. Acknowledge what they've said, and respond with confident humility. Focus less on arguing and more on listening. Look for opportunities to learn and build the relationship.

5. *Make friends and allies through humility.* I learned a fascinating principle from *The Autobiography of Benjamin Franklin.* In 1736, when Franklin was a thirty-year-old printer and newspaper publisher, he was chosen as clerk of the Pennsylvania Assembly. The

term of office was one year. It was a profitable position for Franklin, because he not only received pay for being a member of the assembly, but the province also paid him to print up the paper money and other printed materials issued by the provincial government.

The following year, Franklin was up for reelection and he found himself being opposed and attacked by another member of the assembly. At first, Franklin resented this man's opposition—but he decided that, instead of treating this man as an enemy, he'd find a way to make him a friend. He decided to use a humble approach. Franklin explained:

> *Having heard that he had in his library*
> *a certain very scarce and curious book, I*
> *wrote a note to him, expressing my desire*
> *of perusing that book, and requesting he*
> *would do me the favour of lending it to*
> *me for a few days. He sent it immediately,*
> *and I return'd it in about a week with*
> *another note, expressing strongly my sense*
> *of the favour. When we next met in the*
> *House, he spoke to me (which he had never*
> *done before), and with great civility;*
> *and he ever after manifested a readiness*
> *to serve me on all occasions, so that we*
> *became great friends, and our friendship*
> *continued to his death. This is another*
> *instance of the truth of an old maxim I*

*had learned, which says, "He that has
once done you a kindness will be more
ready to do you another, than he whom
you yourself have obliged." And it shows
how much more profitable it is prudently
to remove, than to resent, return, and
continue inimical proceedings.* [156]

Franklin asked his enemy to do him a favor. To ask a favor, especially of someone who has hurt you and opposed you in the past, is an act of humility. And Franklin's humility changed this man's heart, turning him from an enemy to a friend. Their friendship continued until the man's death.

When we communicate with humility, we turn enemies into friends. It's much easier to achieve our goals of success when we have friends helping us instead of enemies opposing us. Communicate with confidence and humility. You'll be amazed at what you can accomplish.

7

Hire the Humble

Hire people who are willing to learn and have great attitudes.
—Leadership speaker Dan Rockwell

I was hired as general manager of the Spartanburg Phillies in February 1965. I was twenty-five years old, and it was my first-ever job as a sports exec. I had never hired anyone or delegated responsibility before. I needed a secretary, but I didn't know the first thing about hiring a secretary.

I began by running an ad in the "Help Wanted" section of the newspaper. Weeks went by, but no nibbles. Finally, two days before the start of the season, we held an open house at the ballpark so that the public could meet the ballplayers. During the event, a plump, middle-aged lady took me aside and said, "I hear you're looking for a secretary. Is the job still open?"

"Yes, it is, Mrs.—what was your name?"

"Claire Johns. Call me Claire."

"All right, Claire. Tell me, how fast do you type?"

"I don't know. I've never used a typewriter before."

"Do you have good filing and organizational skills?"

"No, not really."

"What kind of office experience *do* you have? Did you ever work as a receptionist?"

"I'm afraid not. I've never worked in an office before."

"Can you be at the office at eight in the morning?"

"I sure can!"

"Congratulations, you've got the job."

In the years since then, I've conducted a lot of job interviews, and I've hired a lot of people for many different jobs—but I don't think I have ever made a smarter decision than hiring Claire Johns as my secretary in the Spartanburg Phillies front office. Her résumé was not very impressive—but she was humble, dedicated, loyal, quick to listen, and eager to learn. Plus, she had a lot of life wisdom to share, and I learned a lot by being her boss. I nicknamed her "Mama Johns," and she was my Gal Friday for four years, and I don't know what I would have done without her.

One of the most important lessons I learned as a young executive I learned by hiring Mama Johns. That lesson is: to build a successful organization, corporation, or team, *hire the humble*.

That lesson, which I discovered at the outset of my executive career, is a lesson many major corporations are coming around to in the twenty-first century.

ARROGANT PEOPLE NEED NOT APPLY

What qualifications do you need to get hired at one of the biggest, most prestigious tech companies in the world? *New York Times* columnist Thomas L. Friedman went to Mountain View, California, and put that question to Laszlo Bock, senior vice president of people operations for Google. Bock said that the standard criteria employers have used over the years are useless. GPAs and test scores, Bock said, "don't predict anything" about a job candidate's future at Google. In fact, he noted, the "proportion of people without any college education at Google has increased over time" and now stands at about 14 percent in many of Google's most critical research and development teams.

This is not to suggest that grades, math skills, computer coding skills, and other academic metrics don't matter. A job applicant's skills are definitely a factor in deciding who gets hired. But there are other qualifications that weigh much more heavily—and one of those qualifications is humility.

The kind of humility Google is looking for is essentially "intellectual humility," the ability to learn from others, learn from experience, and learn from failure; the ability to adapt to new ideas and new situations; the ability to recognize when someone else has a better idea—even when it means discarding our own ideas. "Without humility," said Bock, "you are unable to learn." This is why many graduates from top business schools are shocked to find they are not Google material. Bock explains, "Successful bright people rarely experience failure, and so they don't learn how to learn from that failure."

People who lack humility, he adds, are prone to a "fundamental attribution error." They think that if something goes right, it's because of their own skill and genius; but if something goes wrong, they blame other people or factors beyond their control. Their lack of humility blinds them to the lesson they need to learn from that failure.

The people Bock seeks to hire at Google have that paradoxical balance of confidence plus humility. Google seeks people who will argue fiercely and confidently for their point of view—then, when presented with information that contradicts their view, they will change their minds, humbly and instantly. Thomas Friedman sums it up this way: "You need a big ego and small ego in the same person at the same time."[157] The "big ego/small ego" paradox, of course, is what I call the confidence-humility paradox.

And Google isn't the only company that aggressively hires for humility.

My friend Dwight Bain is an author, speaker, life coach, and radio personality in the Orlando area. He recently took a tour of the Chick-fil-A home office in Atlanta, then he came back and told me about the tour. "Do you know why Chick-fil-A pulled in six billion dollars of revenue last year, in spite of being closed on Sundays?"

I said, "Is it the pickles on the chicken sandwiches?"

"No," Dwight said. "It's the culture of humility and service from the top to the bottom of the organization. A serving heart drives that company. When I took that tour, everybody—and I mean *everybody*—was going out of their way to be helpful to me. If there was anything I needed, I could say the word, and they would get it for me. And if I said, 'Thank you,' they would always respond, 'It's my pleasure.' Chick-fil-A succeeds because everyone in the organization is a humble servant."

Another example is Whole Foods Market, an upscale, all-organic supermarket chain based in Austin, Texas. The company reports annual revenues of around $12 billion, with 431 stores and 91,000 employees around the world. Whole Foods co-CEO Walter Robb gave an interview to *The Wall Street Journal* about his company's hiring philosophy. The *Journal*'s questions were in the form of sentences for Robb to complete. The *Journal*: "'The one trait I look for in new hires is. . ." Robb: "Enthusiasm. Confidence." The *Journal*: "The one trait that won't get you hired is. . ." Robb: "Lack of humility and an over-sense of self-promotion." So, anyone who wants a job at Whole Foods needs to find that harmonious balance of enthusiastic confidence welded to deep humility.

Jayneel Patel, CEO of OpenXCell Technolabs, a mobile app development company, also seeks humility more than ability when interviewing applicants. "The major criteria that I focus on," he says, "while bringing in somebody in my organization is his adapting to our culture rather than being an exceptional performer in solitude. . . . An ideal candidate must consider himself to be smart but shouldn't consider the others around to be idiots. For me that is intellectual humility."[158]

Online shoe and clothing retailer Zappos.com reports a billion dollars in sales annually and regularly ranks high on *Fortune*'s list of "The Best Companies to Work For." Zappos's business model is based on customer loyalty and relationship marketing— especially word-of-mouth recommendations. Excellent service is the key to repeat business. So Zappos places a premium on humility in its employees. The company's slogan is "We are a service company that happens to sell shoes. And handbags. And more. . ." If a company advertises that its product is service, then it needs to have employees with a humble, serving attitude.

CEO Tony Hsieh says that when candidates apply at Las Vegas-based Zappos.com, the interview actually begins on the shuttle that brings the candidates from the airport to corporate headquarters. Zappos hires not merely for ability, but for "cultural fit." The shuttle driver is trained to observe how applicants talk, behave, and treat the driver and other service people. The shuttle driver spends a significant amount of time with the applicants, taking them on a tour of the facility and from one interview to another. At the end of a very full day, the recruiters talk to the driver and get his or her perspective on the applicant.

Hsieh says, "It doesn't matter how well the day of interviews went—if our shuttle driver wasn't treated well, then we won't hire that person." Humility means treating everybody with respect. Arrogant people need not apply.

Hsieh is so confident of the serving culture at Zappos that he once bet a shoe manufacturer's sales rep that he could call the Zappos sales line, and the employee would cheerfully locate the nearest pizza delivery shop. The sales rep placed the call, and the Zappos call center employee came up with a list of five nearby pizza restaurants within two minutes.

Zappos.com doesn't have a book of rules and policies for dealing with every conceivable customer problem. Instead, employees are encouraged to find creative—even extraordinary—solutions to make the customer happy. On one occasion, a call center representative received an unusual request for help with a merchandise return. A woman caller had ordered boots as a gift for her husband—then her husband was killed in a car accident. The call center rep not only facilitated the return for a full refund, but ordered flowers to be delivered to the widow. The rep had full authority to bill the flowers to the company without getting a supervisor's approval.

Tony Hsieh gets emotional when he tells that story, concluding, "At the funeral, the widow told her friends and family about the experience. Not only was she a customer for life, but so were those thirty or forty people at the funeral. Stories like these are being created every single day, thousands and thousands of times. . . . If you get the culture right, then most of the other stuff follows."[159]

Businesses and organizations that nurture a culture of serving and humility have a built-in advantage over those that don't: humility reduces conflict, builds camaraderie, boosts morale, reduces turnover, and improves customer service and satisfaction. A humble workforce tends to increase the bottom line.

To increase the success of your organization, hire the humble.

THE HALF-LIFE OF KNOWLEDGE

Confidently humble people make better leaders, better teachers, better mentors, better coaches, better team players, and better employees. Why? Because people who are both confident and humble are better listeners and better learners. The only way to stay competitive in a fast-changing world is to keep listening—and keep learning.

Are you familiar with "the half-life of knowledge"? This refers to the amount of time that will elapse before half of all knowledge in a particular field becomes obsolete. In *The Half-Life of Facts*, Harvard mathematician Samuel Arbesman cites numerous examples of things we once "knew" as facts that are no longer "true."

For example, science textbooks used to teach that there are forty-eight chromosomes in a human cell; in 1956, researchers discovered that the actual number is forty-six. Doctors used to recommend cigarette smoking to soothe the throat; we now know smoking is deadly. Red meat, notes Arbesman, used to be good for you, then bad for you, then good again, and now it's a toss-up. The same with red wine.

Some "facts," though never proven wrong, have nevertheless changed over time. The speed of computers and the Internet, the population of the earth, and our knowledge of other planets keeps increasing. Our world, our society, our science, and the state of our knowledge are in constant flux. Arbesman explains:

> With our knowledge changing all the time, even the most informed people can barely keep up. All this change may seem random and overwhelming (Dinosaurs have feathers? When did this happen?), but it turns out there is actually order within the shifting noise. This order is regular and systematic and is one that can be described by science and mathematics.
>
> Knowledge is like radioactivity. If you look at a single atom of uranium, whether it's going to decay—breaking down and unleashing its energy—is highly unpredictable. . . . But when you take a chunk of uranium, itself made up of trillions upon trillions of atoms, suddenly the unpredictable becomes predictable. . . .

If we are patient enough, half of
a chunk of uranium will break down
in 704 million years, like clockwork.
This number—704 million years—is
a measurable amount of time, and it is
known as the half-life of uranium.

It turns out that facts, when viewed
as a large body of knowledge, are just as
predictable. Facts, in the aggregate, have
half-lives: We can measure the amount of
time for half of a subject's knowledge to be
overturned.[160]

In the field of medicine, Arbesman adds, half of all knowledge becomes either false or obsolete every forty-five years.[161] In physics, the half-life of knowledge is even shorter, depending on the particular branch of physics: a little over five years in nuclear physics and plasma physics, and about six years in solid-state physics.[162]

There is a half-life of knowledge for every field of human endeavor, from science to medicine to mathematics to economics to history to religion. Human knowledge is not static. It is constantly changing, so we must be committed to continuously learning—and that means we must always be listening and observing. Anyone who is not continuously learning is not keeping up. That's why the humble learner has an advantage over the arrogant know-it-all.

The humble learner must be a reader. The more widely read you are, the greater your fund of knowledge and wisdom. Most successful people are widely read in many fields. They don't confine their curiosity to one small branch of knowledge. They read technical and trade journals. They read newspapers. They read books—both fiction and nonfiction, from the classics to the latest trends.

Humble learners also stay involved by attending seminars and trade conventions in their industry, by volunteering for committees and task forces, by taking classes and even going back to school for an advanced degree. Humble learners are always listening more than they are talking—and they listen to everybody, from leaders and authorities to the receptionist and the janitor. Important information and great ideas can come from anyone, anywhere.

Arrogance produces a kind of blindness and deafness. Humility is a precondition for truly seeing and hearing and understanding. Only the humble truly listen.

A Baylor University study confirms this principle. Dr. Wade Rowatt, associate professor of psychology and neuroscience at Baylor, reports that the study "shows that those who possess the combination of honesty and humility have better job performance. In fact, we found that humility and honesty not only correspond with job performance, but. . .predicted job performance above and beyond any of the other five personality traits like agreeableness and conscientiousness."

The study, published online by the journal *Personality and Individual Differences*, is the first peer-reviewed research to link humility to better job performance. Megan Johnson, the Baylor doctoral candidate who designed the study, talked about the practical implications of these findings. "Honest and humble people could be a good fit for occupations and organizations that require special attention and care for products or clients," she said. "Narcissists, on the other hand, who generally lack humility and are exploitative and selfish, would probably be better at jobs that require self-promotion."[163]

So whether you are a leader, a business owner, an entrepreneur, a manager, a coach, or an employer of any kind, you should recruit humble people who are eager to listen and learn. Yes, look for the talent and experience and competence you need in your business or on your team—but make sure that humility is also one of the top criteria on your list.

And if you are a job applicant, if you are looking for a great employer, a great place to work, a great career where you can achieve your goals and find the success you dream of, first be a person of humility, a listener and a learner. Then seek out an employer who actively recruits humble people. Employers are becoming increasingly aware of the importance of humility as a success trait. Writing in the *Houston Chronicle*, business writer and educator Neil Kokemuller observes:

> *Open-mindedness is one of the most*
> *sought-after employee traits. . . .*
> *Being open-minded means you have a*
> *willingness to listen to other ideas and*
> *opinions and consider the possibility*
> *that you are wrong or may change your*
> *own perspective. . . . Supervisors want*
> *to know that you have a willingness to*
> *learn new things and consider alternative*
> *approaches to problem-solving. In an*
> *interview, showing you are open-minded*
> *instills confidence in the hiring manager*
> *that you are teachable and coachable.*
> *Someone who projects a know-it-all*
> *attitude is often a turn-off.*[164]

Arrogant people think humility equals weakness. Those who are wise know that humility equals strength. A little humility can go a long way toward helping you achieve your goals and dreams.

HUMBLE LEADERS CREATE A CULTURE OF HUMILITY

My friend Dr. Jay Strack, president of Student Leadership University, is a renowned speaker and author. He has spoken at many chapels for various professional sports teams.

When Tony Dungy was head coach of the Tampa

Bay Buccaneers, Jay accepted an invitation to speak at a pregame chapel for the Bucs. Arriving early, Jay went to the room where the chapel would be held and found a man alone in the room, setting up chairs.

"Excuse me," Jay said. "I'm Jay Strack. I'm looking for Coach Dungy."

The man put out his hand and said, "Hi, Jay. I'm Tony. Thanks for coming. I'm setting up the room for you."

"You're Coach Dungy?" Jay was amazed to find the head coach setting up chairs. "Let me help you."

"Actually, I like to set up the chairs myself," Dungy said. "I know where each man sits. I know what each man is going through and where he's hurting—and I pray over each man's chair as I set it up."

That's a glimpse into the deep humility of Coach Tony Dungy. During his coaching career, he managed to motivate his players without screaming and cursing at them. He developed a reputation as a mentor, even a father figure to his players, and it was clear that he loved them and they loved him. Perhaps it is the culture of caring and humility he created that enabled him to amass a career record of 139 wins and 69 losses, plus a championship ring in Super Bowl XLI.

A humble leader builds a culture of humility—and organizations of humility can achieve great things.

Chuck Daly was my friend and a great basketball coach. He coached the Detroit Pistons to back-to-back NBA championships in 1989 and 1990 and coached the United States Men's Olympic Basketball Team to a gold medal at the 1992 Summer Olympics in Barcelona. I became acquainted with Chuck in the late 1970s when I was general manager of the Philadelphia 76ers and Chuck was an assistant coach. We worked together again in the late 1990s when Chuck was head coach of the Orlando Magic. He passed away in 2009.

As a coach, Chuck had that all-important balance of confidence and humility. He was a good listener, and he once told me about a lesson he learned as an assistant with the 76ers.

"Julius Erving came to me shortly after I came aboard as assistant coach," Chuck told me. "He said, 'Do you know where every player on this team wants a shot from?' I had never thought of that before. A lot of coaches design their plays without taking into consideration whether or not a player likes to take a shot from that spot on the court. Ever since Julius pointed that out to me, I've made it a point to find out where each player feels the most comfortable shooting. Then I design plays that will help him get a shooting opportunity from that spot. Julius taught me that insight, and it has made me a better coach."

Coaches only learn from players when they are humble enough to listen. Both sides of the leader-follower equation—coaches and players, employers and employees, teachers and students—need the humility to listen and learn. Good listeners learn from everybody—from those at the top of the organizational chart, and those at the bottom.

Writing in *Harvard Business Review*, leadership consultant John Baldoni, chairman of N2Growth, offers three key insights for hiring the humble and building a culture of humility in the workplace:

"1. Look for signs of humility." When interviewing job applicants, listen carefully to how they describe their accomplishments. Arrogant people take sole credit for their accomplishments and demonstrate a lack of awareness of what it means to collaborate with others. They also tend to shift blame or offer rationalizations for failures.

Humble people share the credit for accomplishments with others. They talk about how they worked in collaboration with other people to solve problems and overcome obstacles. Humble employees contribute to a more harmonious work environment.

"2. Show humility." Leaders should be role models of humility to their followers. If you want to create a culture of humility, set an example of humility. Be quick to listen. Encourage others to share their ideas. People will follow the example you set.

"3. Insist on cooperation." Cooperation only takes place in an atmosphere of mutual respect and humility. We all have strengths and weaknesses, and cooperation involves meshing those strengths and weaknesses in a complementary way. If we let our egos get in the way of our ability to cooperate, teamwork will suffer and we'll fall flat on our faces. But if we practice humility, if we humbly supply what each other lacks, we'll become an unbeatable team.[165]

To enjoy a great career, make humility your lifelong habit. To build a great team or organization, hire the humble.

THE HUMILITY OF TWO SUPERSTARS

In 1976, I had the honor of negotiating the trade that brought Julius Erving—the legendary Dr. J—to the Philadelphia 76ers. He popularized today's above-the-rim style of basketball and is famed for his ability to slam-dunk from the free-throw line. A six-foot-seven forward, he provided firepower and artistry, leading the Sixers to an NBA championship in 1983.

Julius Winfield Erving II was the most recognized athlete of his era. During his glory days with the Sixers, he received fan mail from around the world. The letters were usually addressed to Dr. J, or simply Doc. Despite his worldwide fame, Doc is the most humble and self-effacing athlete I've ever known—and the most confident. He epitomizes that all-important balance of confidence and humility that leads to success.

In 1981, I asked Doc to help put on a basketball clinic at a camp in Schroon Lake, New York. The camp couldn't afford to pay him, but Doc didn't mind. "Don't worry about it," he said. "I'll do it for free."

So in July of that year, I met his flight in Albany and drove him to the camp. During the drive, he told me he had just come from another basketball camp in

Colorado—and he'd had less than four hours' sleep. We took a boat to the island where the camp was held, and the campers had prepared a huge welcome for Doc, with a band, flags, streamers, and a cheering crowd. Though Doc was tired, he gave those campers everything he had and impacted their lives in ways they would never forget.

After the camp, I drove Doc to the airport and thanked him for everything he had done. He humbly waved off my thanks. "It was my privilege," he said.

In August 1982, my wife and I joined Doc and his wife, Turquoise, plus five other NBA stars, for a two-week visit to China. It was an exotic adventure through a land that, a decade earlier, had been closed to Westerners.

One night we stayed in a rural guesthouse near the ancient capital city of Han. The accommodations were primitive—yet there was one very nice room reserved for Doc and Turquoise. Doc came to talk to the rest of us and said, "I'm really not comfortable having the best room in the house. I don't want any special treatment."

But Gene Banks, who played for the San Antonio Spurs, said, "Doc, we want you to have it. Don't feel guilty. You deserve it. You're the reason we're all here. You're a hero to us, and we're happy you're getting some extra attention because of all you've done for us. Take the room and enjoy it."

So, humbly and reluctantly, Doc agreed to spend the night in that room.

At the end of our two-week excursion in China, our entourage arrived in Hong Kong. I phoned the 76ers office in Philadelphia and learned that the Sixers' owner was negotiating a deal to bring Houston Rockets star center Moses Malone to Philadelphia. At first, I felt a little cheated that a major talent acquisition was being made in my absence. But then I realized that our owner had just made the deal of the century. Moses Malone was the best center in the NBA, and we had finally put together everything we needed to win a championship.

At six-foot-ten, Moses was not the tallest center in the game. By most objective measures, he shouldn't have been as great a player as he was. He didn't have the highest vertical leap, the fastest legs, or the most accurate shot. Yet he dominated at his position through hard work, stamina, and competitive attitude. Let other NBA centers have their hook shots and finesse moves—Moses was a "hard hat and lunch pail" player who jackhammered his way to the basket.

A man of few words, Moses frequently spoke of himself in the third person, with statements like, "It's never easy for Moses. Moses got to get out there every night and work hard." *Philadelphia Daily News* writer Phil Jasner once asked Moses what he did during the off-season. Moses replied, "Swim. Pool." Jasner asked, "You got a new swimming pool?" Moses replied, "Nope. Went swimming. Played pool."

One of the big questions was whether Moses might

upset the delicate alchemy of the Philadelphia 76ers. Many sportswriters questioned whether Moses could coexist with the Sixers marquee player, Julius Erving—or whether he might bring a big ego into the Sixers locker room, disrupting team chemistry.

We introduced Moses Malone at a press conference on September 15, 1982. These events are usually conducted in a suit and tie, but Moses appeared before the press in a plain brown shirt and Levis—humble attire that spoke volumes about his humble attitude.

When a reporter asked Moses how he would get along with Julius Erving, he replied, "This is Doc's show, and it's always been a great show. Moses is just here to help Doc. And I think it's gonna be an even better show."

And Moses meant it. There was no clash of egos. In fact, I can't remember a team before or since in which there was so much talent, so much confidence, yet so much humility expressed by its two superstars, Julius Erving and Moses Malone.

As a result, the Philadelphia 76ers amassed a regular-season record of 65 and 17 and went on to win the NBA championship—and win it convincingly. We swept the Knicks, then beat the Milwaukee Bucks in five, then swept the Lakers for the title. Our humble, hardworking, lunch pail center, Moses Malone, was named playoffs MVP.

We had a big celebration parade down Broad Street in Philadelphia. Crowds lined the street, cheering and celebrating as our players waved from parade floats. As the float bearing Moses Malone passed by a construction site, about a dozen construction workers in hard hats stood in unison and hoisted their lunch pails in a salute to Moses Malone, a lunch pail player.

I was deeply saddened when Moses passed away in his sleep at age sixty, the night before he was to play in a charity golf tournament in Virginia.

Dr. J and Moses were two of the greatest players I've ever known—and amazingly, two of the most humble men I've ever known. When our team hired these two confident yet self-effacing megastars to play basketball in Philadelphia, we thought we were hiring great talent—and we were right. What we didn't realize at the time was that we were also hiring great humility. And it was that unbeatable combination of great talent and great humility that brought a championship to Philadelphia.

If you want to achieve great things, if you want to build a successful organization, take my advice. Hire the humble.

8

Humility—a Learnable Skill

Humility is the fear of the LORD;
its wages are riches and honor and life.
—King Solomon of Israel (Proverbs 22:4)

Franklin Delano Roosevelt, the hero of the poor and working class during the Great Depression, was born to wealth and privilege. His speeches and policies helped define the American spirit during the first half of the twentieth century. Our world was indelibly stamped by his presidency and his personality.

FDR was born on January 30, 1882, in Hyde Park, New York, the son of a politically well-connected businessman, James Roosevelt. When Franklin was four or five, his father took him to the White House to meet President Grover Cleveland. The president shook hands with young Franklin and said, "I have one wish for you, little man, that you will never be president of the United States."[166]

Franklin attended Harvard College, where he became editor-in-chief of *The Harvard Crimson*. During his college years, Franklin's fifth cousin, Theodore Roosevelt, was elected president of the United States. In 1905, Franklin married his fifth cousin once removed, Eleanor Roosevelt (yes, Roosevelt was both her maiden name and married name). Eleanor's uncle,

President Theodore Roosevelt, gave the bride away.

FDR was elected to the New York State Senate in 1910 and served as assistant secretary of the navy under Woodrow Wilson from 1913 to 1920. He was the vice presidential running mate of Ohio Governor James M. Cox in the 1920 presidential election, but Cox lost to Warren G. Harding. The summer after that loss, Franklin and Eleanor and their five children vacationed in the summer home they owned on Campobello Island in New Brunswick. They went sailing, swimming, and sunning on the beach.

During this vacation, Franklin was stricken with chills, fever, and muscle aches. He lost strength in his left leg. A local doctor diagnosed him with the flu. But as the numbness in his legs continued to spread, Eleanor sent for a specialist, Dr. Robert Lovett, who recognized Franklin's condition immediately: FDR had polio. He would be paralyzed from the waist down for the rest of his life.[167]

Frances Perkins, one of Franklin Roosevelt's long-time friends, watched him go through his agonizing illness. She had known him before he was stricken with polio and continued to be a close friend and adviser afterward (as president, Roosevelt appointed her secretary of labor). The pre-polio FDR had all the arrogance of a young New York blue blood, born to wealth and social superiority. But his paralysis changed him. In her memoirs, Frances Perkins described how Roosevelt's affliction affected his character:

Franklin Roosevelt underwent a spiritual transformation during the years of his illness. I noticed when he came back that the years of pain and suffering had purged the slightly arrogant attitude he had displayed on occasion before he was stricken. The man emerged completely warmhearted, with humility of spirit and with a deeper philosophy. Having been to the depths of trouble, he understood the problems of people in trouble. . . .

He was young, he was crippled, he was physically weak, but he had a firmer grip on life and on himself than ever before. He was serious, not playing now. . . .

I began to see what the great teachers of religion meant when they said that humility is the greatest of virtues, and that if you can't learn it, God will teach it to you by humiliation. Only so can a man be truly great, and it was in those accommodations to necessity that Franklin Roosevelt began to approach the stature of humility and inner integrity which made him truly great.[168]

FDR's grandson Curtis later wrote that Roosevelt's affliction "provided the one thing we all need, deep frustration, that keen sense that you cannot do everything you want to do. The only thing that mattered to FDR [before his illness]. . .was his political ambition, and to have it thrown in his face that it looked impossible must have entered into his soul."[169] FDR's disability humbled him, increased his compassion for others, and made him stronger as a leader and a human being.

Roosevelt possessed that special quality of supreme confidence tempered by humility that tends to produce great leadership. He had the self-assurance to make difficult decisions, and to make them firmly, without second-guessing himself. He once told a friend, "At night when I lay my head on my pillow, and it is often pretty late, and I think of the things that have come before me during the day and the decisions that I have made, I say to myself—well, I have done the best I could and turn over and go to sleep."[170]

We see both the confidence and the humility of Roosevelt in an incident that took place in 1936. One of the largest of FDR's New Deal jobs programs was the Public Works Administration, headed by Secretary of the Interior Harold Ickes. There were many political turf battles within the Roosevelt administration, and Ickes was frequently at odds with other members of the Roosevelt administration. When a May 1936 newspaper story suggested that Ickes's days in the administration were numbered, Ickes stormed into the Oval Office and accused the president of siding with his enemies and plotting to get rid of him.

"Harold," Roosevelt admonished, "you're being childish."

The hotheaded Ickes turned and left without apology.

Later, after taking time to cool down and think rationally, Ickes realized he had behaved like a fool—and had undoubtedly destroyed his White House career. He recorded his thoughts in his journal: "I responded hotly. I never thought I would talk to a president of the United States the way I talked to President Roosevelt last night."

An arrogant leader would have fired Ickes for his disrespect and insubordination. But Roosevelt, in his humility, understood what drove Ickes to say what he said. He knew that Ickes had a fiery temper—and he thought it would do the man good to suffer for a while. But he also knew that Ickes was too good a man to lose.

A few days later, FDR reprimanded Ickes in a cabinet meeting. Harold Ickes was humiliated—and he was sure the reprimand in front of his peers signaled that he was soon to be fired. So he went to his office, typed up an angry resignation letter, signed it, and sent it to the president.

The next day, Harold Ickes was in the White House dining room, picking at his lunch but not feeling very hungry. He looked up and saw President Roosevelt approaching in his wheelchair. Without a word, the president handed Ickes a handwritten letter which read in part, "Dear Harold. . . I have *full* confidence in you

. . . . You are needed to carry on a big common task . . . . Resignation *not* accepted! Your affectionate friend, Franklin D. Roosevelt."

One sign of authentic humility is the ability to empathize with others, to accept them with all their faults and foibles, and to restore them to useful service when they have failed. FDR demonstrated a tough-yet-tender compassion, rooted in the lessons of humility he learned during his affliction with polio. As a result of Roosevelt's wise and humble handling of the situation, Harold Ickes learned an important lesson. He later reflected, "What could a man do with a president like that! Of course I stayed."[171]

Franklin Delano Roosevelt started out as an arrogant young man—born to wealth and privilege, narcissistic and self-important. He learned humility when he suffered the life-changing, paralyzing effects of the polio virus. Arrogant people don't often become humble until they are humbled.

But we don't have to wait until we are humbled by circumstances. We can change—if we want to change. We can *choose* to become humble, because humility, like arrogance, is a choice.

How to Be Humble

In these pages, I have offered story after story, proof after proof, that *humility is the secret ingredient of success*. And humility is a learnable skill. Let me offer some suggestions in how to *choose* humility and how to *acquire the skill* of being authentically humble.

1. *Make a decision to stop defending yourself and justifying yourself.* When you defend yourself, you are really defending your ego and pride. Lower your defenses and people will notice—and what they will notice is humility in action.

Try taking responsibility and blame even when it's someone else's fault. For example, if your customer angrily and unreasonably blames you for something that is actually his fault, try saying, "I understand how you feel. I will take full responsibility for this mistake, and I will make it right." If your spouse blames you for an argument you're having, try saying, "I don't blame you for feeling that way. I take full responsibility for the misunderstanding. How can I make it up to you?"

2. *Make a point of sharing credit and praising others.* Every day, make sure you give credit or praise to someone in your family, someone on your team, someone in your organization. Be specific, be gracious, and above all, be sincere. No empty flattery—just honest recognition and appreciation.

One of the best ways of sharing credit and praise is to say good things about people behind their backs. Most of us find it easy to criticize, judge, and spread gossip about other people behind their backs. But humble people don't tear other people down; they build people up. Humble people don't destroy reputations; they enhance reputations. So find good things to say about people behind their backs, and imagine how good they will feel when your kind, positive words get back to them.

3. *Practice putting yourself in other people's shoes.* Make a habit of empathizing with others. Ask yourself, "What must it be like to be him, with the problems he's facing?" Or, "What must it be like to be her, after I just reprimanded her in front of her peers?" Only the humble are able to see a situation through another person's eyes—and only the humble even want to.

When other people do things that are baffling to you, ask questions and try to understand their point of view. Try to figure out what motivates them, what hurts them, what excites them, what pleases them. Instead of dismissing the feelings and emotions of other people, try to understand why they feel the way they do—then show compassion to them.

Take a sincere interest in other people. Seek out shy people, and invite them to join the conversation. Ask them questions, and listen attentively to their answers. Avoid interrupting. Instead of trying to impress other people, work on discovering who they really are—their plans and goals, their interests and concerns, their wants and needs. Until you are able to empathize with other people and see the world through their eyes, you'll never achieve authentic humility.

4. *Surrender the right to be judgmental.* Let's be careful with this word *judgment*. There are certain kinds

of judgment that are essential to our lives. For example, we should exercise good judgment (discernment) when making decisions.

What I mean when I talk about *being judgmental* is viewing others as socially, morally, or spiritually inferior to ourselves. We judge other people because of the clothes they wear, their political views, their social status, their economic status, and on and on. Usually we judge others based on partial, even sketchy information. We think we know the facts when in reality we know next to nothing about the people we judge. Being judgmental is presumptuous—and arrogant.

Why are we so judgmental toward other people? We often try to raise ourselves up by putting others down. The pleasure of being judgmental is the experience of feeling superior to other people. It's the guilty pleasure of arrogance. You cannot be humble and judgmental at the same time. Authentic humility cancels out judgment.

Humble people have no reason or motivation to judge others. They would much rather try to understand and empathize. Humble people are too busy working on their own flaws to point out the flaws of others.

Notice when you look down on people for any reason—and make a conscious decision to replace judgment with acceptance and understanding. The more conscious you are of your tendency to judge others, the less you will do it—and the more humble you will become.

5. *Serve others.* Serve your family members, your boss, your employees, your teammates, your neighbors, and even strangers. As much as possible, do your serving in secret. Serving others in order to get recognition only feeds your ego. Instead, serve in humility by serving anonymously. Try to do good things for others without getting caught.

Serve the people who, according to society's rules, ought to be serving you. Serve your subordinates and employees. Do good things for other people who can't do anything for you. Serve others, expecting nothing in return. Tutor a child, volunteer at a homeless shelter, mow the lawn or wash windows for your elderly neighbor. Find a way to become a servant to others—and that lifestyle of serving will begin to change you from the inside out.

Shortly before Christmas 2005, Coach Tony Dungy's eighteen-year-old son James took his own life. It was a devastating loss, a parent's worst nightmare. A few weeks after James died, a man came to Coach Dungy and said, "My son's fiancée recently committed suicide. Now my son is depressed and he talks about ending his own life. Could you call him and find a way to help him?"

So Coach Dungy called the young man and said, "My name is Tony. Your dad asked me to talk to you." Tony told the young man how much he had suffered after his son James took his own life. "You know, son," he concluded, "I don't know why God allowed my son to die. But maybe it was so that I could talk to you and tell you, 'Don't do that to your daddy.'" Then he asked the young man to call him in the morning, and the young man promised he would.

Coach Dungy talked to this young man by phone every day for a week. Finally, the young man said he was doing better, and he promised not to take his own life. Then the young man asked, "Tony, what do you do for a living?"

"I'm a football coach," Dungy replied.

"College or high school football?"

"I coach the Indianapolis Colts," Tony said.

Only then did this young man realize he'd been talking to Coach Tony Dungy. An arrogant person might have tried to impress this young man. But Coach Dungy was only interested in serving this young man and saving his life. That's humility in action.

6. *Master the art of the apology.* Arrogant people find it hard to apologize. Admitting they are wrong feels like killing a part of themselves—their false image of perfection. Humble people are aware of their own flaws, and they don't hesitate to confess their errors. Arrogant people have no use for forgiveness—and feel no need to be forgiven. Humble people know the liberating feeling of being forgiven.

So when you hurt or offend someone, be quick to apologize. Don't offer excuses or mitigating circumstances. Simply say, "I was wrong. I'm sorry. Please forgive me." Once you have mastered the art of the apology, you are well on your way to acquiring the life skill of humility.

Permit me to tell a couple of embarrassing stories on myself. The first took place in the late 1970s, when I was the general manager of the Philadelphia 76ers. Our starting guard Doug Collins had an ongoing battle with stress fractures in the bones of his feet. While talking to a Philadelphia sports writer about Doug's latest foot injury, I said, "Doug obviously has a low pain threshold." The reporter quoted me in print— and Doug showed up at my desk.

"What right do you have to talk to the media about my pain threshold?" he said.

I instantly realized I had spoken carelessly. Being susceptible to fractures is not at all the same thing as having a "low pain threshold." Doug was angry—and he had every right to be. The fact that he played many games in pain with his feet and ankles taped up was proof that he played admirably through pain. I had blown it—big time.

"Doug," I said, "you're right—I was out of line. I apologize. Please forgive me. Believe me, I've learned a lesson, and it will never happen again." And it didn't— and Doug graciously accepted my apology.

The second embarrassing story: In June 1997, I flew to Detroit to speak to a group of automotive executives. A limo driver was supposed to meet me at the airport but never showed. After an hour of waiting, I arrived at my hotel, where a trainee desk clerk was taking forever, helping another customer. It was late, I was tired, and I became impatient. I proceeded to make a big show of my disgruntlement—pacing, sighing, and muttering.

Finally, the man ahead of me was registered, so I stepped up to the desk—and the clerk said, "Just a moment, sir—I'll be right with you." So I heaved a big sigh and waited some more.

The man who had registered ahead of me paused and said to me, "It's not the clerk's fault. He's new, and he's a little nervous and he's doing the best he can. Your huffing and puffing isn't going to make him go any faster. I suggest that next time you try a little patience."

Oof! The man was right, and I had that coming. I had behaved like a jerk.

Before I could say anything, the man turned and headed for the elevator. The thought occurred to me: *What if that guy is in the audience for my speech tomorrow?*

Just then, the clerk returned—and I went out of my way to make amends for my earlier rudeness.

The next morning I came out of my room and headed for the elevator—and when the elevator doors opened, there was my friend, who had lectured me on patience. "We meet again," he said, smiling pleasantly.

"I'm glad we did," I said. "I want to apologize. You were right—the way I behaved was inexcusable." And we had a nice chat for a few moments, then we went our separate ways. I had learned an important lesson in patience and humility—and I got a chance to practice the art of the apology.

On His Feet or on His Knees

Stephen Curry, the phenomenal shooting guard for the Golden State Warriors, has been called by many sports analysts the greatest shooter in NBA history. In the 2014–15 season, Curry earned NBA Most Valuable Player honors while leading the Warriors to their first championship since 1975. The following season, Steph Curry became the first NBA player to be elected MVP by unanimous vote. The Warriors won seventy-three games, breaking the record (set by Michael Jordan and the 1995–96 Chicago Bulls) for most wins in an NBA regular season.

Steph is the son of retired NBA star Dell Curry, the Charlotte Hornets' all-time leader in points (9,839) and three-point field goals made (929). Steph played college basketball at Davidson in North Carolina. His college coach, Bob McKillop, recalls that the young Steph Curry he coached "had no fear of failure. If he missed a shot, missed five shots, he didn't care. It didn't disrupt him. It didn't destroy his focus. He knew he was going to make the next five. . . . You find me a pro athlete today that can have that balance between humility and confidence that he has and I'll be shocked."[172]

There it is again: Steph Curry's college coach is amazed at his former star player's "balance between humility and confidence." It's proof once more (as if any additional proof is needed) that great confidence plus deep humility produces amazing success. All of Curry's fame and success, all the praise of the sports writers and the acclaim of the crowds is like water off a duck's back. Steph Curry always seems to wear that same sweet smile, and when he speaks, he speaks gently and humbly.

On February 25, 2016—in fact, as this book was being written—the Golden State Warriors came to Orlando for their one appearance of the year. Steph and the Warriors are the hottest thing in sports, and the game was an absolute sellout. The building was packed to the rafters—and it seemed there were almost as many fans wearing Steph Curry jerseys as fans wearing Orlando Magic gear. It was a madhouse. The Curry Craze was on full display.

Before every game, there's a chapel service for the players of both teams. I decided to attend. I slipped in a little late, and there was only one chair available. The chaplain was already delivering a brief homily for the players. There were about fourteen players, representing both teams. The noise from the arena filtered faintly into the room. Though it was raucous out in the arena, in this little chapel room, the atmosphere was quiet and reflective.

As I took the empty chair, I looked to my left—and there sat Stephen Curry. The chaplain finished speaking, then nodded to me and said, "We have Pat Williams with us today, who started the first NBA chapels when he was general manager of the 76ers. I'm going to ask Pat if he would close in prayer."

(Credit where credit is due: NBA chapels were actually the idea of Bobby Jones, who played forward for the 76ers from 1978 to 1986. Bobby, a humble servant if there ever was one, brought the idea to me, and together we started the first NBA chapels, and they soon spread throughout the league.)

I agreed to give the prayer, and the chaplain said, "Are there any prayer requests?" Two players asked for prayer. Then, as I was about to pray, Steph Curry said, "I think we should all kneel."

So we all got down on our knees—fourteen Magic and Warriors players and one NBA exec—and without anyone suggesting it, we all automatically reached out and joined hands. Steph Curry took my left hand in his right hand, and we joined our hearts in prayer to God.

At the conclusion of the prayer, we all rose, shook hands, and spoke words of blessing and friendship to one another.

Then Steph Curry, in his humble-confident way, went out into our arena and proceeded to light us up for 51 points. He shot ten three-pointers, and the Golden State Warriors steamrolled the Magic, 130 to 114.

The fans saw Stephen Curry's amazing talent and confidence on the court. But I was grateful that I had also seen Steph Curry's amazing humility. Whether he's on his feet or on his knees, Steph Curry is a role model of humble confidence. I'm convinced that his deep humility is the secret ingredient of his success. And that same secret ingredient is available to you and me.

During my senior year at Tower Hill School in Wilmington, Delaware, I was quarterback of the football team and my friend, Ruly Carpenter, was our star running back. On two different drives during a late-season game against archrival Wilmington Friends School, we moved the ball to our opponents' one yard line. On both of those drives, we had first-and-goal situations, and I was tempted to call a quarterback sneak. It would have been so easy to dive into the end zone behind the center—and I could just see my name in the morning headlines

But at the same time, I thought of my friend Ruly, the highly recruited all-state running back. If I made the touchdown, I might gain a little glory—but I would be stealing some of the recognition Ruly had earned that season. And he might see it as a betrayal of our friendship.

I had a few moments of indecision — but ultimately, I cared more about the team and our friendship then I did about making those touchdowns. So both times, I called Ruly's number—then I took the snap and handed off to Ruly. Both times he punched the ball into the end zone.

The final score was Tower Hill 40, Wilmington Friends 7—and we sealed an undefeated season. I knew

Ruly would get the headline the next morning—and I was happy for him.

Looking back, I think that is one of the first times in my sports career I chose humility over selfishness. And I knew I had made the right choice. The rightness of my choice was reaffirmed after the game. I was in the locker room, changing into my street clothes, when our assistant coach, Baird Brittingham, walked up. "Pat," he said, "I believe you can play college football."

That was an eye-opener. No coach had ever said that to me before. As it turned out, I would play baseball, not football, when I went on to Wake Forest University. But it meant the world to me that Coach Brittingham saw that potential in me. I don't think he said that because of my play-calling or my pass completions. I think he said I could play college ball because, in those first-and-goal situations, I had chosen humility over personal glory. I had made decisions based on what was best for the team.

During that game, I discovered that humility is not just a trait you're born with. Humility is a learnable skill. And humility is a choice.

So make that choice. Then go out and confidently, humbly pursue your goals.

Epilogue

Humble Greatness

*There will always be a reason why you meet people.
Either you need them to change your life or
you're the one who will change theirs.*
—Novelist Madeline Sheehan

In the fall of 2011, my daughter Karyn called me and said, "Dad! I have a surprise for you—someone wants to say hi!"

Moments later, I heard another voice—a voice I instantly recognized as that of celebrated ESPN announcer Stuart Scott. Stuart and I had become friends in the early 1990s when he was working at WESH-TV in Orlando. It was clear that he was headed for the big time, and sure enough, it wasn't long before Stuart was anchoring ESPN's *SportsNight* and appearing regularly on *SportsCenter*.

We chatted for a few minutes, and it was great to catch up with Stuart. We exchanged numbers so we could stay in better touch. I didn't find out until later how Karyn had happened to run into Stuart.

Karyn was on St. George Island, off the Florida Panhandle, for a weekend beach trip with some of her girlfriends. They decided to go out to eat on their first night there, and soon after they were seated, they started hearing whispers from nearby patrons:

"Ohmigosh, isn't that Stuart Scott?" "Where? No way! It's him!" Karyn's ears perked up. She remembered meeting Stuart when she was twelve or thirteen and he was an Orlando sports anchor. She looked around and spotted him a few tables away.

Though Karyn didn't expect Stuart to remember her after almost twenty years, she remembered the lesson I always taught my children: never be afraid to go up and introduce yourself to famous people. I've told them, "There are no giants out there—just people who have worked hard to get where they are. Don't be intimidated. Talk to them and learn from them. You'll find that the greatest people usually have a very humble spirit."

She waited until Stuart had finished his meal, and then she took her ol' dad's advice. She got up, went to his table, and said, "Hi, Stuart. I don't know if you remember me or not, but I'm Karyn Williams. My dad is Pat Williams with the Orlando Magic."

Karyn expected Stuart to politely shake her hand and say, "Good to see you. Tell your dad hi for me."

Instead, Stuart jumped up and shouted, "*Little Williams!*" And he gave her a big hug. Karyn was amazed.

"Of course I remember you! It's so good to see you! How are your brothers, Jimmy and Bobby? And the rest of your family? And how's your dad doing? I've been wanting to call him and encourage him in his cancer battle, but I don't have his number."

He was kind and effusive, and Karyn was amazed. It was as if Stuart was a long-lost family member. They chatted for a few moments, then Karyn got out her phone, called me, and put Stuart on the line.

Stuart Scott was one of the most recognizable personalities in sports television—and the fact that Stuart and Karyn happened to encounter each other in a tiny restaurant on a tiny island so far from where either of them lived was an incredible coincidence—

If you believe in coincidence.

But the point of this story is the way Stuart responded. He could have "big timed" my daughter and politely but firmly brushed her off. Instead, he was kind and genuine and yes, humble.

Karyn visited with Stuart for a while that night, and he opened up to her about his own cancer battle. In 2007, a sudden bout of abdominal cramps indicated a bad appendix. But when doctors removed the appendix, they found it to be cancerous. He underwent a series of surgeries and chemotherapy. His cancer went into remission for a while, but as he told Karyn, it returned in 2011. That was the same year I was diagnosed with multiple myeloma.

As soon as Karyn got back home, she mailed Stuart one of her CDs with an encouraging note about a song called "Rest in the Hope" that she had written after my diagnosis with multiple myeloma. After Stuart heard the song, he tweeted about it to his two million Twitter followers, then wrote Karyn privately and asked if she would talk to his daughters. They were having a hard time emotionally with their dad's cancer battle, an issue Karyn understood all too well.

Karyn maintained contact and a sweet friendship with Stuart and his family.

Stuart went through endless rounds of chemo in 2014, plus radiation and more surgeries. Finally, on January 4, 2015, we received word that Stuart's unforgettable voice had gone silent. His humble fighting spirit, however, lives on and continues to inspire us.

I have always tried to teach my children that people are what matter in this world. I'm not in the basketball business. Karyn is not in the music business. Stuart was not in the broadcasting business. We are all in the people business. And no matter how successful we become, we should never be too big or too famous or too busy to share our lives with the people we encounter along the way. Stuart was a gracious, kind, humble human being, and that's what made him great.

So be a great human being, my friend. Humbly take time for people.

The challenge of leadership is to be strong, but not rude; be kind, but not weak; be bold, but not a bully; be thoughtful, but not lazy; be humble, but not timid; be proud but not arrogant; have humor, but without folly.
—Entrepreneur and speaker Jim Rohn

Contact

You can contact Pat Williams at:
Pat Williams
c/o Orlando Magic
8701 Maitland Summit Boulevard
Orlando, FL 32810
phone: 407-916-2404
pwilliams@orlandomagic.com
Visit Pat Williams's website at:
www.PatWilliams.com

If you would like to set up a speaking engagement for Pat Williams, please call or write his assistant, Andrew Herdliska, at the above address, or call him at 407-916-2401. Requests can also be faxed to 407-916-2986 or e-mailed to aherdliska@orlandomagic.com.

We would love to hear from you. Please send your comments about this book to Pat Williams at the above address. Thank you.

Notes

¹ Steve Twomey, "A Pioneer with Courage, Influence and Humility," *Washington Post,* July 18, 2001, https://www.washingtonpost.com/archive/politics/2001/07/18/a-pioneer-with-courage-influence-and-humility/5b1aa5aa-87fa-4b7e-b494-66ffa4051ad1/.

² Ibid.

³ John C. Danforth, "Homily" (sermon text, funeral of Katharine Graham, Washington National Cathedral, June 23, 2001), http://www.cathedral.org/worship/sermonTexts/jcd010623.shtml.

⁴ Dave Goldiner, "Tiger Woods' Mistress Scandal Costs Shareholders of Sponsors like Nike, Gatorade $12 Billion," *New York Daily News,* December 29, 2009, http://www.nydailynews.com/news/tiger-woods-mistress-scandal-costs-shareholders-sponsors-nike-gatorade-12-billion-article-1.432269.

⁵ Joe Pompeo, "The Price of Tiger Woods' Ex-Wife's Silence: $750 Million and Custody of the Kids," *Business Insider,* June 30, 2010, http://www.businessinsider.com/the-price-of-tiger-woods-wifes-silence-750-million-and-custody-of-the-kids-2010-6; Vicki Walker and Randy McMullen, "Tiger Woods Pays $750 Million in Divorce Settlement, Report Says," Denver Post, June 30, 2010, http://www.denverpost.com/spencer/ci_15413568.

⁶ Mike Freeman, "Woods Shows Arrogance in Hogan Comparison," CBS News, April 10, 2010, http://www.cbsnews.com/news/woods-shows-arrogance-in-hogan-comparison/.

⁷ David A. Kaplan, "Tyco's 'Piggy,' Out of Prison and Living Small," *New York Times,* March 1, 2015, http://www.nytimes.com/2015/03/02/business/dealbook/dennis-kozlowskis-path-from-infamy-to-obscurity.html?_r=0.

⁸ Daniel Schorn, "Dennis Kozlowski: Prisoner 05A4820: Morley Safer Speaks with the Ex-Tyco Chief Behind Bars," CBS News, March 22, 2007, http://www.cbsnews.com/news/dennis-kozlowski-prisoner-05a4820/.

⁹ Ibid.

¹⁰ Steve Forbes and John Prevas, P*ower Ambition Glory: The Stunning Parallels between Great Leaders of the Ancient World and Today—and the Lessons You Can Learn* (New York: Crown Business, 2009), 104–5.

¹¹ John Crumpacker, "Figure Skater Kwan Dismisses Longtime Coach," SFGate.com, October 25, 2001, http://www.sfgate.com/sports/article/Figure-skater-Kwan-dismisses-longtime-coach-2864575.php.

¹² C. S. Lewis, *The Screwtape Letters* (New York: HarperCollins, 2001), 69–70.

¹³ Donovan Campbell, *The Leader's Code: Mission, Character, Service, and Getting the Job Done* (New York: Random House, 2013), 42.

¹⁴ Ibid., 42–44.

¹⁵ Jeff Stafford, "George Stevens: A Filmmaker's Journey," Turner Classic Movies, January 2012, http://www.tcm.com/this-month/article/236927%7C0/

George-Stevens-A-Filmmaker-s-Journey.html.

[16] David J. Bobb, *Humility: An Unlikely Biography of America's Greatest Virtue* (Nashville, TN: Thomas Nelson, 2013), 11.

[17] Gabriel Moran, *Living Nonviolently: Language for Resisting Violence* (Lanham, MD: Lexington Books, 2011), 60.

[18] Harry S. Truman, *Off the Record: The Private Papers of Harry S. Truman*, ed. Robert H. Ferrell (Columbia, MO: University of Missouri Press, 1997), 287.

[19] George Washington, "Letter to Lewis Nicola," May 22, 1782, TeachingAmericanHistory.org, http://teachingamericanhistory.org/library/document/letter-to-lewis-nicola/.

[20] Matthew Spalding, "The Man Who Would Not Be King," Heritage.org, February 5, 2007, http://www.heritage.org/research/commentary/2007/02/the-man-who-would-not-be-king.

[21] Robert Leckie, *George Washington's War: The Saga of the American Revolution* (New York: HarperCollins, 1992), 140; Mark Lardas, *George Washington: Leadership, Strategy, Conflict* (Oxford: Osprey, 2011), 11.

[22] "George Washington Biography," Biography.com, A&E Television Networks, 2014, http://www.biography.com/people/george-washington-9524786.

[23] David McCullough, "The Glorious Cause of America" (assembly address, Brigham Young University, September 27, 2005), http://speeches.byu.edu/reader/reader.php?id=10804.

[24] A. K. Fielding, "George Washington: The Humble Statesman," Western Journalism, February 19, 2013, http://www.westernjournalism.com/george-washington-the-humble-statesman/.

[25] "George Washington Biography," Biography.com.

[26] James C. Rees with Stephen J. Spignesi, *George Washington's Leadership Lessons: What the Father of Our Country Can Teach Us about Effective Leadership and Character* (Hoboken: Wiley, 2007), 78.

[27] John Emory Godbey and Allen Howard Godbey, *Light in Darkness; or, Missions and Missionary Heroes* (St. Louis, MO: Holoway & Co., 1887), 304.

[28] Creative Commons, "Laozi" (Lao-Tzu), Wikiquote.org, October 28, 2015, https://en.wikiquote.org/wiki/Laozi.

[29] Andrew Murray, *Humility and Absolute Surrender* (Peabody, MA: Hendrickson Publishers, 2005), 11.

[30] Owen Collins, ed., *Speeches That Changed the World* (Louisville, KY: Westminster John Knox Press, 1998), 32.

[31] Alexander K. McClure, *Lincoln's Yarns and Stories* (Chicago & Philadelphia: John C. Winston Co., 1901), Project Gutenberg Edition, http://www.gutenberg.org/files/2517/2517-h/2517-h.htm. [Some dialogue paraphrased for

the sake of clarity.]

[32] Ibid.

[33] Abraham Lincoln, "Short Autobiography—1859," ibid.

[34] Mario M. Cuomo and Harold Holzer, *Lincoln on Democracy* (New York: Fordham University Press, 2004), 105–6.

[35] Clifton Fadiman and André Bernard, eds., *Bartlett's Book of Anecdotes* (New York: Little Brown, 2000), 347.

[36] McClure, *Lincoln's Yarns and Stories.*

[37] David Herbert Donald, *Lincoln* (New York: Simon & Schuster, 1995), 576.

[38] James M. McPherson, *Battle Cry of Freedom: The Civil War Era* (New York: Oxford University Press, 1988), 846–47.

[39] Richard Wightman Fox, " 'A Death-shock to Chivalry, and a Mortal Wound to Caste': The Story of Tad and Abraham Lincoln in Richmond," *Journal of the Abraham Lincoln Association,* Summer 2012, http://quod.lib.umich.edu/j/jala/2629860.0033.203/--death-shock-to-chivalry-and-a-mortal-wound-to-caste?rgn=main;view=fulltext.

[40] Clint Johnson, *Pursuit: The Chase, Capture, Persecution, and Surprising Release of Confederate President Jefferson Davis* (New York: Kensington, 2009), Kindle edition.

[41] Fadiman and Bernard, *Bartlett's Book of Anecdotes,* 349; McClure, *Lincoln's Yarns and Stories.*

[42] Russell Razzaque, "Political Intelligence: Learning Humility from Lincoln," *Psychology Today,* April 10, 2012, https://www.psychologytoday.com/blog/political-intelligence/201204/learning-humility-lincoln.

[43] Constance Victoria Briggs, *The Encyclopedia of God: An A-Z Guide to Thoughts, Ideas, and Beliefs about God* (Charlottesville, VA: Hampton Roads Publishing Company, 2003), 87.

[44] George Orwell, *George Orwell: In Front of Your Nose, 1946–1950* (Jaffrey, NH: Nonpareil, 2000), 465.

[45] Ibid., 111.

[46] Ibid., 113–14.

[47] Emma Tarlo, *Clothing Matters: Dress and Identity in India* (Chicago: University of Chicago Press, 1996), 76–78.

[48] Amit Goswami with Richard E. Reed and Maggie Goswami, *The Self-Aware Universe: How Consciousness Creates the Material World* (New York: Jeremy P. Tarcher, 1995), 264–65. [Some dialogue paraphrased for greater clarity.]

[49] Orwell, *In Front of Your Nose,* 463.

[50] Frank Luksa, "Humble Hunt Never Afraid to Think Big," ESPN.go.com, December 14, 2006, http://espn.go.com/nfl/news/story?id=2697048.

⁵¹ ESPN.com News Services, "Thoughts and Reactions on Lamar Hunt," ESPN.go.com, December 15, 2006, http://espn.go.com/nfl/news/story?id=2697075.

⁵² Christie Smythe and Keri Geiger, "Shkreli, Drug Price Gouger, Denies Fraud and Posts Bail," Bloomberg.com, December 17, 2015, http://www.bloomberg.com/features/2015-martin-shkreli-securities-fraud/.

⁵³ Rebecca Robbins, "The Martin Shkreli Show: The Widely Scorned Pharma Exec Just Can't Stop Talking," STAT News, November 12, 2015, https://www.statnews.com/2015/11/12/martin-shkreli-show-reviled-pharma-exec-just-cant-stop-talking/.

⁵⁴ Sarah Ferris, "Smirking Drug CEO Antagonizes Lawmakers after Pleading the Fifth," The Hill, February 4, 2016, http://thehill.com/policy/healthcare/268190-martin-shkreli-pleads-fifth-in-first-appearance-on-hill.

⁵⁵ Carolyn Y. Johnson, " 'Pharma Bro' Shkreli Stays Silent before Congress, Calls Lawmakers 'Imbeciles' in Tweet," *Washington Post*, Wonkblog, February 4, 2016, https://www.washingtonpost.com/news/wonk/wp/2016/02/04/pharma-bro-martin-shkreli-faces-congress-today-but-pledges-silence/.

⁵⁶ Ahiza Garcia, "Martin Shkreli's E*Trade Account Takes a Huge Hit," CNN Money, February 3, 2016, http://money.cnn.com/2016/02/03/news/martin-shkreli-bail-bond-value/.

⁵⁷ John Marzulli and Meg Wagner, " 'Pharma Bro' Martin Shkreli, Detested CEO Who Jacked Up Price of AIDS Pill, Arrested on Securities Fraud Charges," *New York Daily News*, December 17, 2015, http://www.nydailynews.com/news/national/martin-shkreli-detested-pharma-ceo-arrested-report-article-1.2468546.

⁵⁸ Zachary Crockett, "The Art of Handling a PR Implosion," Priceonomics.com, September 25, 2015, http://priceonomics.com/the-art-of-handling-a-pr-implosion/.

⁵⁹ Ken Blanchard and Scott Blanchard, "Don't Let Your Ego Hijack Your Leadership Effectiveness," *Fast Company*, June 22, 2012, http://www.fastcompany.com/1840932/dont-let-your-ego-hijack-your-leadership-effectiveness.

⁶⁰ HP Alumni, "The HP Way," Hewlett-Packard Alumni Association, Inc., HPAlumni.org, http://www.hpalumni.org/hp_way.htm.

⁶¹ Jim Collins, "The 10 Greatest CEOs of All Time," *Fortune*, July 21, 2003, http://www.jimcollins.com/article_topics/articles/10-greatest.html.

⁶² Jim Collins, "Foreword," from *The HP Way* by David Packard, JimCollins.com, May 2005, http://www.jimcollins.com/article_topics/articles/the-hp-way.html.

⁶³ Various authors, "Bill & Dave Stories," HPMemoryProject.org, http://hpmemoryproject.org/timeline/stories/bill_and_dave_00.htm.

⁶⁴ Ibid.

[65] Ibid.

[66] Yi Che Wu, "Steve Jobs on Picking Up the Phone, on Asking, and on Failure" (video posted on YouTube.com, January 9, 2012), https://www.youtube.com/watch?v=CThPfG9ag9E.

[67] Dave Packard, "Dave Packard's 11 Simple Rules," IESE Alumni Magazine, University of Navarra (Pamplona, Spain), http://www.ee-iese.com/92/word_porras.htm.

[68] Marie Stempinski, "Best CEOs Have Humble Streak," *Tampa Bay Times*, May 19, 2013, http://www.tampabay.com/news/business/workinglife/best-ceos-have-humble-streak/2121406.

[69] Mark H. McCormack, *What They Still Don't Teach You at Harvard Business School* (New York: Bantam, 1989), 112.

[70] Dan Price, "Gravity Payments CEO Dan Price Reflects on $70 K Minimum Salary Experiment and Its Aftermath," Today.com, December 30, 2015, http://www.today.com/series/2015-voices/gravity-payments-ceo-dan-price-reflects-70k-minimum-salary-experiment-t64401.

[71] Paul Keegan, "Here's What Really Happened at That Company That Set a $70,000 Minimum Wage," *Inc.*, November 2015, http://www.inc.com/magazine/201511/paul-keegan/does-more-pay-mean-more-growth.html.

[72] Michele Manelis, "Michael Keaton: From Batman to Birdman," *New Zealand Herald,* January 8, 2015, http://www.nzherald.co.nz/entertainment/news/article.cfm?c_id=1501119&objectid=11383054.

[73] Jonathan Pearson, *Next Up: 8 Shifts Great Young Leaders Make* (Chicago: Moody, 2014), Kindle edition.

[74] C. S. Lewis, *Mere Christianity* (New York: HarperCollins, 2001), 128.

[75] *Christian Post* staff, "James Caviezel of 'Passion' Interviewed," ChristianPost.com, February 18, 2004, http://www.christianpost.com/news/james-caviezel-of-passion-interviewed-4749/.

[76] Chris Seay, *The Gospel According to Lost* (Nashville, TN: Thomas Nelson, 2009), 93.

[77] Charles R. Swindoll, *Growing Strong in the Seasons of Life* (Grand Rapids, MI: Zondervan, 2007), 271.

[78] Michael Lewis, "Don't Eat Fortune's Cookie," Princeton University's 2012 Baccalaureate Remarks, June 3, 2012, https://www.princeton.edu/main/news/archive/S33/87/54K53/.

[79] Roderick M. Kramer, "The Harder They Fall," *Harvard Business Review,* October 2003, https://hbr.org/2003/10/the-harder-they-fall.

[80] Rheana Murray, "Mayor Rob Ford's Most Outrageous One-Liners," ABC News, May 1, 2014, http://abcnews.go.com/International/mayor-rob-fords-outrageous-liners/story?id=23548022.

[81] Brian M. Harward, *Presidential Power: Documents Decoded* (Santa Barbara, CA: ABC-CLIO, 2016), 153–54.

[82] Ronald Reagan, *The Last Best Hope: The Greatest Speeches of Ronald Reagan* (West Palm Beach, FL: Humanix, 2016), 204–5.

[83] R. W. Apple, Jr., "The Reagan White House; in a Spirit of Contrition Reagan's Concession on Iran Affair Evokes Memories of Kennedy's Bay of Pigs Speech," *New York Times,* March 5, 1987, http://www.nytimes.com/1987/03/05/us/reagan-white-house-spirit-contrition-reagan-s-concession-iran-affair-evokes.html.

[84] Eric Nicol, *Script Tease: A Wordsmith's Waxings on Life and Writing* (Toronto: Dundurn Press, 2010), 229.

[85] Nelson Mandela, *Long Walk to Freedom: The Autobiography of Nelson Mandela* (New York: Back Bay Books, 1995), 19.

[86] Ibid., 21.

[87] Kharunya Paramaguru, "5 Great Stories about Nelson Mandela's Humility, Kindness, and Courage," Time.com, December 6, 2013, http://world.time.com/2013/12/06/5-great-stories-about-nelson-mandelas-humility-kindness-and-courage/.

[88] Nelson Mandela, "I Am Prepared to Die" (defense statement in the Rivonia Trial, April 20, 1964), Nelson Mandela Foundation, http://db.nelsonmandela.org/speeches/pub_view.asp?pg=item&ItemID=NMS010.

[89] Nelson Mandela, "Nelson Mandela's Address to a Rally in Cape Town on His Release from Prison," February 11, 1990, African National Congress, http://www.anc.org.za/show.php?id=4520.

[90] Paramaguru, "5 Great Stories."

[91] Ibid.

[92] André Brink, "Mandela a Tiger for Our Time," *The Guardian,* May 22, 1999, http://www.theguardian.com/world/1999/may/22/nelsonmandela.weekend7.

[93] Del Jones, "Music Director Works to Blend Strengths," *USA Today,* October 27, 2003, http://usatoday30.usatoday.com/educate/college/careers/profile9.htm.

[94] Jim Collins, "Level 5 Leadership: The Triumph of Humility and Fierce Resolve," *in Business Leadership: A Jossey-Bass Reader,* 2nd ed., ed. Joan V. Gallos (San Francisco: Jossey-Bass, 2008), 99–100.

[95] Michael Maccoby, "Narcissistic Leaders: The Incredible Pros, the Inevitable Cons" (reprinted from 2000), *Harvard Business Review,* January 2004, https://hbr.org/2004/01/narcissistic-leaders-the-incredible-pros-the-inevitable-cons.

[96] Michael Maccoby, *The Productive Narcissist: The Promise and Peril of Visionary Leadership* (New York: Broadway Books, 2003), 6.

[97] Maccoby, "Narcissistic Leaders"; Michael Maccoby, "Why People Are Drawn

to Narcissists like Donald Trump," *Harvard Business Review,* August 26, 2004, https://hbr.org/2015/08/why-people-are-drawn-to-narcissists-like-donald-trump.

[98] Maccoby, *The Productive Narcissist,* 7–8.

[99] McClure, *Lincoln's Yarns and Stories.*

[100] Maccoby, *The Productive Narcissist,* 151–52.

[101] Abraham Lincoln, "To Norman B. Judd," in *Collected Works of Abraham Lincoln,* vol. 3, ed. Roy P. Basler, The Abraham Lincoln Association, University of Michigan, http://quod.lib.umich.edu/l/lincoln/lincoln3/1:39?rgn=div1;view=fulltext.

[102] J. B. McClure, *Anecdotes & Stories of Abraham Lincoln: Early Life Stories, Professional Life Stories, White House Stories, Miscellaneous Stories* (Mechanicsburg, PA: Stackpole Books, 2006), 199.

[103] Ibid., 200–202.

[104] Ibid., 40.

[105] Gautam Mukunda, "Abraham Lincoln, Poster President for the Great Leadership Paradox," *Fast Company,* September 14, 2012, http://www.fastcompany.com/3001249/abraham-lincoln-poster-president-great-leadership-paradox.

[106] Mayo Clinic Staff, "Narcissistic Personality Disorder: Symptoms," MayoClinic.org, November 18, 2014, http://www.mayoclinic.org/diseases-conditions/narcissistic-personality-disorder/basics/symptoms/con-20025568.

[107] Maccoby, "Narcissistic Leaders."

[108] Henry Blackaby and Richard Blackaby, *Called to Be God's Leader: How God Prepares His Servants for Spiritual Leadership* (Nashville, TN: Thomas Nelson, 2004), 37.

[109] Maccoby, "Narcissistic Leaders."

[110] John Mather, M.D., "Myth: Churchill's Speech Impediment Was Stuttering," The Churchill Centre, http://www.winstonchurchill.org/learn/myths/myths/he-stuttered.

[111] Harold Begbie, *The Mirrors of Downing Street* (New York: GP Putnam's Sons, 1921), http://www.gutenberg.org/files/15306/15306-h/15306-h.htm.

[112] Keith Sharp, "Winston Churchill, Stutterer," Utstat.UToronto.ca, November 30, 2012, http://www.utstat.utoronto.ca/sharp/Churchill.htm.

[113] Winston Churchill, "The War Situation: House of Many Mansions" (broadcast, London, January 20, 1940), The Churchill Centre, http://www.winstonchurchill.org/learn/speeches/speeches-of-winston-churchill/98-the-war-situation-house-of-many-mansions.

[114] Winston Churchill, "Blood, Toil, Tears and Sweat" (first speech as Prime Minister to House of Commons, May 13, 1940), The Churchill Centre, http://www.winstonchurchill.org/learn/speeches/speeches-of-winston-churchill/92-

blood-toil-tears-and-sweat.

[115] Norman Rose, Churchill: *The Unruly Giant* (New York: Free Press, 1994), 322–23.

[116] Gary Shapiro, "How Churchill Mobilized the English Language," *New York Sun*, June 12, 2012, http://www.nysun.com/new-york/how-churchill-mobilized-the-english-language/87862/.

[117] Max Domarus, *The Essential Hitler: Speeches and Commentary*, ed. Patrick Romane (Wauconda, IL: Bolchazy-Carducci, 2007), viii.

[118] Jerrold M. Post, *The Psychological Assessment of Political Leaders* (Ann Arbor, MI: University of Michigan Press, 2003), 86–87.

[119] Fadiman and Bernard, *Bartlett's Book of Anecdotes*, 123.

[120] Winston Churchill, "This Is Your Victory" (speech, Ministry of Health, London, May 8, 1945), The Churchill Centre, http://www.winstonchurchill. org/learn/speeches/speeches-of-winston-churchill/123-this-is-your-victory. [Compared and corrected against the BBC audio recording at http://www. archive.org/download/Winston_Churchill/1945-05-08_BBC_Winston_ Churchill_VE_Day_Celebrations_Ministry_of_Health_Building.mp3.]

[121] BBC, "On This Day: 30 November—1954: Winston Churchill Turns 80," BBC.co.uk, November 30, 2005, http://news.bbc.co.uk/onthisday/hi/dates/ stories/november/30/newsid_3280000/3280401.stm.

[122] Richard Langworth, *Churchill by Himself: The Definitive Collection of Quotations* (New York: Public Affairs, 2008), 516, 519.

[123] Norman McGowan, *My Years with Churchill* (New York: British Book Centre, 1958), 15–16.

[124] Ibid., 19.

[125] Ibid., 55.

[126] Ibid., 18.

[127] Ibid., 137–38.

[128] Ibid., 142.

[129] Ibid., 139–40.

[130] Jeanine Prime and Elizabeth Salib, "The Best Leaders Are Humble Leaders," *Harvard Business Review*, May 12, 2014, https://hbr.org/2014/05/the-best-leaders-are-humble-leaders.

[131] Pat Williams with Dave Wimbish, *How to Be Like Coach Wooden: Life Lessons from Basketball's Greatest Leader* (Deerfield Beach, FL: Health Communications, Inc., 2006), 15.

[132] John Wooden, "Confidence—John R. Wooden's Pyramid of Success #14," Earn Purple Blog, June 25, 2013, http://earnpurpleinc.blogspot.com/2013/06/

confidence-john-r-woodens-pyramid-of.html.

[133] Earle Rice Jr., *George S. Patton* (Philadelphia, PA: Chelsea House, 2004), 110–11.

[134] Porter B. Williamson, *General Patton's Principles for Life and Leadership*, 5th ed. (Tucson, AZ: Management & Systems Consultants, 2015), 3.

[135] Robert G. Torricelli and Andrew Carroll, *In Our Own Words: Extraordinary Speeches of the American Century* (New York: Pocket Books, 1999), 140–42.

[136] Alan Axelrod, *Patton on Leadership: Strategic Lessons for Corporate Warfare* (Paramus, NJ: Prentice Hall, 1999), 43.

[137] John J. Pitney Jr., *The Art of Political Warfare* (Norman, OK: University of Oklahoma Press, 2001), 58.

[138] Benjamin Franklin, *The Autobiography of Benjamin Franklin*, ed. Charles W. Eliot (New York: P. F. Collier & Son, 1909), Gutenberg.org, http://www.gutenberg.org/files/148/old/bfaut11.txt.

[139] Ibid.

[140] Ralph Louis Ketcham, *The Political Thought of Benjamin Franklin* (Indianapolis: Hackett Publishing, 2003), l–li.

[141] Paul Kengor, "That Wall," *National Review*, June 12, 2007, http://www.nationalreview.com/article/221231/wall-paul-kengor.

[142] Ronald Reagan, *An American Life* (New York: Simon and Schuster, 1990), 706–7.

[143] Michael Reagan, *Lessons My Father Taught Me: The Strength, Integrity, and Faith of Ronald Reagan* (West Palm Beach, FL: Humanix Books, 2016), 126–27.

[144] Ibid., 129.

[145] Ibid., 133.

[146] Ibid., 134.

[147] Maria Bartiromo with Catherine Whitney, *The 10 Laws of Enduring Success* (New York: Crown, 2010), 24.

[148] John Bussey, "How Women Can Get Ahead: Advice from Female CEOs," *Wall Street Journal*, May 18, 2012, http://www.wsj.com/articles/SB10001424052702303879604577410520511235252.

[149] Joyce Purnick, "Mother Teresa Gains Release of Three Prisoners," *New York Times*, December 25, 1985, http://www.nytimes.com/1985/12/25/nyregion/mother-teresa-gains-release-of-3-prisoners.html; Associated Press, "Mother Teresa Wants State to Release AIDS Prisoners," *New York Times*, January 3, 1986, http://www.nytimes.com/1986/01/03/nyregion/mother-teresa-wants-state-to-release-aids-prisoners.html; King Duncan, *The Amazing Law of Influence* (New York: Pelican, 2001), 193; Robert Palestini, *Feminist Theory and Educational Leadership: Much Ado about Something!* (Lanham, MD: Rowman

& Littlefield, 2013), 119; Dale Carnegie, Stuart R. Levine, and Ross Klavan, *The Leader in You,* book excerpt, SimonAndSchuster.com, http://books. simonandschuster.com/Leader-in-You/Stuart-R-Levine/9780743549240/ excerpt. [Some sources for this anecdote indicated that three prisoners were released, others said four prisoners. *The New York Times* listed three prisoners by name, so the authors believe three to be the accurate number.]

150 Joseph Langford, *Mother Teresa's Secret Fire: The Encounter That Changed Her Life, and How It Can Transform Your Own* (Huntington, IN: Our Sunday Visitor, 2008), 44.

151 King Duncan, *The Amazing Law of Influence* (New York: Pelican, 2001), 193.

152 Palestini, *Feminist Theory,* 118–19.

153 Father Dwight Longenecker, "The Day I Met Mother Teresa," Patheos.com, September 5, 2007, http://www.patheos.com/blogs/standingonmyhead/2007/09/ the-day-i-met-mother-teresa.html.

154 John C. Maxwell, *Good Leaders Ask Great Questions: Your Foundation for Successful Leadership* (New York: Hachette, 2014), 33.

155 Larry King, "Larry King in Quotes," *The Telegraph,* December 16, 2010, http://www.telegraph.co.uk/culture/tvandradio/8207302/Larry-King-in-quotes.html.

156 Franklin, *The Autobiography of Benjamin Franklin.*

157 Thomas L. Friedman, "How to Get a Job at Google," *New York Times,* February 22, 2014, *Sunday Review,* New York edition, SR11.

158 Jayneel Patel, "Intellectual Humility: The New Hiring Criteria of the World," LinkedIn.com, October 28, 2014, https://www.linkedin.com/ pulse/20141028122733-40661050-intellectual-humility-the-new-hiring-criteria-of-the-world.

159 Max Chafkin, "The Zappos Way of Managing," *Inc.*, May 1, 2009, http://www. inc.com/magazine/20090501/the-zappos-way-of-managing_pagen_4.html.

160 Samuel Arbesman, T*he Half-Life of Facts: Why Everything We Know Has an Expiration Date* (New York: Penguin, 2012), 2–3.

161 Ibid., 30.

162 Ibid., 32.

163 Baylor Media Communications, "New Baylor Study Shows Higher Job Performance Linked to People Who Are More Honest and Humble," Baylor University, March 1, 2011, https://www.baylor.edu/mediacommunications/ news.php?action=story&story=89350.

164 Neil Kokemuller, "Is It Important to Be Open-Minded in the Workplace?" Work.Chron.com, http://work.chron.com/important-open-minded-workplace-6124.html.

[165] John Baldoni, "Use Humility to Improve Performance," *Harvard Business Review,* November 5, 2009, https://hbr.org/2009/11/use-humility-to-improve-perfor/.

[166] John Gunther, *Roosevelt in Retrospect: A Profile in History* (New York: Harper, 1950), 168.

[167] David M. Oshinsky, *Polio: An American Story* (New York: Oxford University Press, 2005), 24–26.

[168] Frances Perkins, *The Roosevelt I Knew* (New York: Penguin, 2011), 29–30; 44–45.

[169] Joseph E. Persico, *Franklin and Lucy: President Roosevelt, Mrs. Rutherfurd, and the Other Remarkable Women in His Life* (New York: Random House, 2008), 187.

[170] Doris Kearns Goodwin, "Franklin D. Roosevelt," Character Above All, PBS. org, http://www.pbs.org/newshour/spc/character/essays/roosevelt.html.

[171] Paul F. Boller, Presidential Anecdotes (New York: Oxford University Press, 1996), 269-270; Gil Troy, *Leading from the Center: Why Moderates Make the Best Presidents* (New York: Basic Books, 2008), 106–7.

[172] Cory Collins, "Stephen Curry Started Small, but He's Always Been Big-Time," *The Sporting News,* April 27, 2015, http://www.sportingnews.com/nba/news/stephen-curry-high-school-golden-state-warriors-nba-playoffs/v3t7j5f9zncm1xt7pzap2h5ua.